The
A to Z Guide
to Bible Application

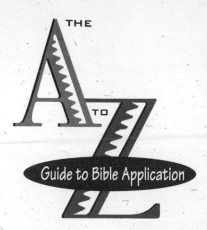

THE A TO Z

Guide to Bible Application

This Billy Graham Evangelistic Association
special edition is published with permission
from Tyndale House Publishers.

Tyndale House Publishers, Inc.
WHEATON, ILLINOIS

Life Application is a registered trademark of Tyndale House Publishers, Inc.

Developed for Tyndale House by The Livingstone Corporation: Linda K. Taylor, James C. Galvin, and Bill Sanders, project staff.

Scripture quotations marked NASB are taken from the New American Standard Bible, © 1960, 1962, 1963, 1968, 1971, 1972, 1973, 1975, 1977 by The Lockman Foundation. Used by permission.

Scripture quotations marked NIV are taken from the Holy Bible, New International Version®. NIV®. Copyright © 1973, 1978, 1984 by International Bible Society. Used by permission of Zondervan Publishing House. All rights reserved.

Scripture quotations marked "NKJV" are taken from the New King James Version. Copyright © 1979, 1980, 1982 by Thomas Nelson, Inc. Used by permission. All rights reserved.

Scripture quotations marked NRSV are taken from the New Revised Standard Version of the Bible, copyrighted, 1989 by the Division of Christian Education of the National Council of the Churches of Christ in the United States of America, and are used by permission. All rights reserved.

The publisher gratefully acknowledges the role of Youth for Christ/USA in preparing the Life Application Notes.

Originally published as The Student's A to Z Guide to Bible Application

ISBN 0-913367-86-9

CONTENTS

How to Get Started

If you're like most people, the Bible probably doesn't seem like a book that you can just sit down and read. Much of the Bible may seem hard to follow or difficult to understand. But remember this: The Bible is actually a collection of sixty-six books. These books were written in different styles and with different purposes. Some of them read like stories. Others were written as poetry. Four of the books (the Gospels) are biographies of Jesus. Proverbs is a collection of wise thoughts. God creatively used these different genres to make the Bible a very special book. But learning to use such a tool requires practice, much like learning to play the piano or the guitar. We may envy someone who plays well and tell ourselves we want to play as well as they, but without practice, our desire will only be a wish. So the more we learn to use the Bible, the more useful it will become to us. That's what this Guide is all about—helping people learn to use the Bible.

Very often people come to the Bible for answers to specific questions. They want to find out what God says about a certain area of life. They want a solution to a problem they are facing. The Bible has answers to many of these questions, but it wasn't written like a typical answer book. For many people, this makes the Bible very difficult to use. To help solve this problem, this Guide has been written to connect your questions directly with answers from God's Word. It isn't a substitute for the Bible, but it will help you make better use of your Bible.

Once you begin studying the Bible, you will soon notice one very important fact: We don't think like God. Our way of doing things isn't usually God's way (look up Isaiah 55:8 for a comment from God on this matter). So reading God's Word forces you to decide whether or not you will obey God. For instance, many people think that the excuse "everybody is doing it" justifies any behavior. The Bible makes it clear, however, that God commands us to obey even if *no one else* seems willing (2 Corinthians 6:16-18).

As you learn to obey God, you will soon discover that the Creator of life knows best how life should be lived. You will also find your mind gradually changing, becoming more like God's. Because you are focusing on God's thoughts, you will begin to think the same way he does. In the book of Romans there is a powerful description of how this works:

Therefore, I urge you, brothers, in view of God's mercy, to offer your bodies as living sacrifices, holy and pleasing to God—this is your spiritual act of worship. Do not conform any longer to the pattern of this world, but be transformed by the renewing of your mind. Then you will be able to test and approve what God's will is—his good, pleasing and perfect will.

Romans 12:1-2, NIV

This Guide will help you . . . but you still have to practice!

How to Use This Guide

The A to Z Guide to Bible Application will help you discover what the Bible has to say on more than one hundred important topics. Each topic includes several Bible readings with Life Application notes, plus many more passages in the Bible that you can look up.

Using this guide is easy. Think about a topic that relates to a question you have or a particular situation you are facing. For example, let's say you've just gotten into a verbal battle with someone and you're not sure what to do. You can turn to topics like *ANGER, FOR-GIVENESS, FRIENDSHIP, PEACE*, etc. These topics will lead you to Bible passages and then provide notes to help you understand them.

Make sure you pay attention—especially if what you read challenges what you have been thinking. God may be trying to change your mind! But also make sure you go beyond reading—put what you learn into action. The point here isn't to find out who knows the most Bible material. Listen to the warning James wrote:

Do not merely listen to the word, and so deceive yourselves. Do what it says.

James 1:22, NIV

The process may be awkward at first—like trying any new skill. But God will honor your effort if you practice.

ABORTION

Is It Just an Easy Solution?

Bible Reading: Psalm 139:1-24

Key Verses: *For it was you who formed my inward parts; you knit me together in my mother's womb.* Psalm 139:13, NRSV

Few issues are as volatile as abortion—the removal of an embryo or fetus from a woman's body in order to end a pregnancy. The pro-abortion and pro-life camps are each convinced of the rightness of their own positions. But what does God say about abortion? While no Bible verse speaks specifically about it, there are Bible passages that give principles that apply to this difficult topic. In Psalm 139, David praises God for overseeing his life, starting before he was born. Because God is the Creator and Designer of all life, it is a logical conclusion that no one should treat that life lightly. Yet, tragically, abortion has become simply a means of birth control, of removing an unwanted complication. If you or a friend is faced with an unwanted pregnancy, you would be wise to read the Bible passages listed here and then seek the advice and wisdom of someone you trust. Abortion may end a problem, but it also ends a life.

If you or a friend has had an abortion and feels guilty, remember that God forgives your sins. If you seek him and ask his forgiveness, he promises to answer your prayer.

CHECK IT OUT:

Genesis 1:26. *We are made in God's image.*
Genesis 4:8-10. *Innocent blood calls to God.*
Exodus 1:15-21. *God detests the killing of infants.*
2 Chronicles 28:2-5. *God judges nations that kill children.*
Isaiah 49:1, 5. *We are called and known by God.*
Jeremiah 16:17. *God sees everything, including abortions.*

Mark 9:36-37. *Welcoming children is welcoming Christ.*
Luke 18:15-17. *Jesus welcomed children.*

ACHIEVEMENTS

The End Doesn't Justify the Means

Bible Reading: Genesis 27:1-46

Key Verses: *[Rebekah said to Jacob,] "Go now to the flock and bring me two choice kids from there, that I may prepare them as a savory dish for your father. . . . Then you shall bring it to your father . . . , so that he may bless you before his death."* Genesis 27:8-10, NASB

When Rebekah learned that Isaac was preparing to bless Esau, she quickly devised a plan to trick him into blessing Jacob instead. Although God had already told her that Jacob would become the family leader (25:23-26), Rebekah took matters into her own hands. She resorted to doing something wrong to try to bring about what God had already said would happen. For Rebekah, the end justified the means. But no matter how good we think our goals are, we should not follow Rebekah's example and attempt to achieve our goals by doing what is wrong.

Rely on God First

Bible Reading: Joshua 7:1-26

Key Verse: *Then Joshua tore his clothes, and fell to the earth on his face before the ark of the LORD until evening, he and the elders of Israel; and they put dust on their heads.* Joshua 7:6, NKJV

When Joshua first went against Ai, he did not consult God but relied on the strength of his army to defeat the small city. Only after Israel was defeated did they turn to God and ask, "What happened?" Too often we rely on our own skills and strength, especially when the task before us seems easy. We go to God only when the obstacles seem too great. However, only God knows what lies ahead. Consulting him first, even when we are on a winning streak, may save us from grave mistakes or misjudgments.

Share Your Vision

Bible Reading: Nehemiah 2:1-18

Key Verse: *And I told them how the hand of my God had been favorable to me, and also about the king's words which he had spoken to me. Then they said, "Let us arise and build." So they put their hands to the good work.*

Nehemiah 2:18, NASB

Nehemiah had a vision, and he shared it with enthusiasm, inspiring Jerusalem's leaders to rebuild the walls.

Spiritual renewal often begins with one person's vision. But sometimes those who receive a vision underestimate people and don't challenge others with their dreams for God's work in the world. Don't see yourself as the only one through whom God is working. Often God uses one person to express the vision and others to turn it into reality. When God plants an idea in your mind to accomplish something for him, share it with others and trust the Holy Spirit to fill them with similar desires.

Don't Rest on Your Laurels

Bible Reading: Nehemiah 6:15–7:4

Key Verse: *And I said to them, "Do not let the gates of Jerusalem be opened until the sun is hot; and while they stand guard, let them shut and bar the doors; and appoint guards from among the inhabitants of Jerusalem, one at his watch station and another in front of his own house."*

Nehemiah 7:3, NKJV

The wall was complete, but the work was not finished. Nehemiah assigned each family the task of protecting the section of wall next to their home. It is tempting to relax our guard and rest on past accomplishments after we have completed a large task. But we must continue to work, serve, and care for all that God has entrusted to us. Following through after a project is completed is as vital as doing the project itself.

Remember the Source

Bible Reading: Hosea 12:1-14

Key Verse: *Ephraim has said, "Ah, I am rich, I have gained wealth for myself; in all of my gain no offense has been found in me that would be sin."* Hosea 12:8, NRSV

Rich people and nations often claim that their material success is due to their own hard work, initiative, and intelligence. Because they have every possession they want, they don't feel the need for God. They believe that their riches are their own, and they feel they have the right to use them any way they please. When you find yourself feeling proud of your material success, remember that all your opportunities, abilities, and resources come from God and that you hold them in sacred trust for him.

CHECK IT OUT:

Genesis 11:1-9. *We must glorify God.*
Joshua 1:6-9. *Success is obeying God.*
Psalm 1:1-3. *Those who delight in God's law will prosper.*
Ecclesiastes 4:4. *Don't let envy be your motivation for success.*
Mark 10:42-45. *Serve others.*
1 Corinthians 9:24-27. *Run straight to the goal.*
Philippians 3:12-21. *Keep focusing on your goals.*
James 4:13-16. *Make sure your goals please God.*

(see also Success)

ANGER

Is It Ever OK to Be Angry?

Bible Reading: Numbers 25:1-13

Key Verses: *The LORD said to Moses, "Phinehas son of Eleazar, the son of Aaron, the priest, has turned my anger away from*

the Israelites; for he was as zealous as I am for my honor
among them, so that in my zeal I did not put an end to
them."   Numbers 25:10-11, NIV

It is clear from Phinehas's story that some anger is
proper and justified. But how can we know when our
anger is appropriate and when it should be restrained?
Ask these questions when you become angry: (1) Why
am I angry? (2) Whose rights are being violated (mine or
another's)? (3) Is the truth (a principle of God) being violated? If only your rights are at stake, it may be wiser to
keep angry feelings under control. But if the truth is at
stake, anger is often justified, although violence and
retaliation are usually the wrong way to express it (Phinehas's case was unique). If we are becoming more and
more like God, we should be angered by sin.

Let God Guide Your Anger

Bible Reading: 1 Samuel 11:1-15

Key Verses: *And the spirit of God came upon Saul in power when he*
heard these words, and his anger was greatly kindled. He
took a yoke of oxen, and cut them in pieces and sent
them throughout all the territory of Israel by messengers,
saying, "Whoever does not come out after Saul and
Samuel, so shall it be done to his oxen!" Then the dread
of the LORD fell upon the people, and they came out as
one.   1 Samuel 11:6-7, NRSV

Anger is a powerful emotion that is often misused to
hurt others. But anger directed at sin and the mistreat-
ment of others is not wrong. Saul was angered by the
Ammonites' threat to humiliate and mistreat his fellow
Israelites. God used Saul's anger to bring justice and
freedom. When injustice or sin makes you angry, ask
God how you can channel that anger in constructive
ways to help bring about a positive change.

Anger's Dangers

Bible Reading: Matthew 5:17-26

Key Verse: *But I tell you that anyone who is angry with his brother* *will be subject to judgment. Again, anyone who says to his brother, "Raca," is answerable to the Sanhedrin. But anyone who says, "You fool!" will be in danger of the fire of hell.*   Matthew 5:22, NIV

Killing is a terrible sin, but anger is a great sin too because it also violates God's command to love. Anger in this case refers to a seething, brooding bitterness against someone. It is a dangerous emotion that always threatens to leap out of control, leading to violence, emotional hurt, increased mental stress, and other destructive results. It can cause spiritual damage as well by keeping us from developing a spirit that is pleasing to God. Have you ever been proud that you didn't strike out and say what was really on your mind? Self-control is good, but Christ wants us to practice thought-control as well. Jesus said we will be held accountable even for our attitudes.

How Anger Can Help

Bible Reading: Mark 3:1-5

Key Verse: *And when He had looked around at them with anger, being grieved by the hardness of their hearts, He said to the man, "Stretch out your hand." And he stretched it out, and his hand was restored as whole as the other.*
                                        Mark 3:5, NKJV

Jesus was angry about the Pharisees' uncaring attitudes. His example teaches us that anger itself is not wrong. Rather, it's how we respond to our anger that may be wrong. Too often we express our anger in selfish and harmful ways. By contrast, Jesus expressed his anger by correcting a problem—healing the man's hand. Follow Jesus' example, and use your anger to find constructive solutions rather than to add to the problem by tearing people down.

CHECK IT OUT:

Genesis 4:6-8. *Anger can lead to murder.*
Numbers 20:1-12. *Anger can have devastating results.*
Numbers 22:29. *Pride often causes anger.*
1 Kings 21:4-10. *Anger can lead to hatred and revenge.*

Psalm 13. *Tell God when you're angry.*

Proverbs 19:19. *A bad temper will get you into trouble.*

John 2:14-16. *We should be angry about those things that displease or insult God.*

Romans 1:18-20. *God makes his anger toward the wicked known.*

Ephesians 4:26. *Don't carry a grudge.*

James 3:5-6. *Don't speak in anger.*

APPEARANCE

More than Good Looks

Bible Reading: Genesis 24:1-27

Key Verse: *And the girl was very beautiful, a virgin, and no man had had relations with her; and she went down to the spring and filled her jar, and came up.* Genesis 24:16, NASB

Rebekah had physical beauty, but the servant was looking for a sign of inner beauty. Our appearance is important to us, and we spend time and money improving it. But how do we develop our inner beauty? Patience, kindness, and joy are the beauty treatments that help us become truly lovely on the inside.

God Looks at Your Character

Bible Reading: 1 Samuel 16:1-13

Key Verse: *But the LORD said to Samuel, "Do not consider his appearance or his height, for I have rejected him. The LORD does not look at the things man looks at. Man looks at the outward appearance, but the LORD looks at the heart."* 1 Samuel 16:7, NIV

King Saul was tall and handsome; he was an impressive-looking man. Samuel may have been trying to find someone who looked like Saul to be Israel's next king, but God warned him against judging by appearance alone. But appearance doesn't reveal what people are really like or their true value. When people judge by outward appearance, they may overlook quality individuals who simply lack the particular physical qualities society currently admires.

Fortunately, God judges by character, not appearances. While we spend hours each week maintaining our outward appearance, we should do even more to develop our inner character. Everyone can see your face, but only you and God know what your heart really looks like. Which is the more attractive part of you?

Ugly on the Inside

Bible Reading: 1 Samuel 30:21–31:13

Key Verse: *Then Saul said to his armorbearer, "Draw your sword, and thrust me through with it, lest these uncircumcised men come and thrust me through and abuse me."*
1 Samuel 31:4, NKJV

Saul was tall, handsome, strong, rich, and powerful. But all of this was not enough to make him someone we should copy. He was tall physically, but he was small spiritually. He was handsome, but his sin made him ugly. He was strong, but his lack of faith made him weak. He was materially rich, but he was spiritually bankrupt. He could give orders to many, but he couldn't command their respect or allegiance. Saul looked good on the outside, but he was decaying on the inside. Godly character is much more valuable than good looks. Work on being more Christlike rather than being more physically attractive.

Noticed by Whom?

Bible Reading: Isaiah 3:12-26

Key Verse: *The LORD said: . . . The daughters of Zion are haughty and walk with outstretched necks, glancing wantonly with their eyes, mincing along as they go, tinkling with their feet.* Isaiah 3:16, NRSV

The women of Judah had placed their emphasis on clothing and jewelry rather than on God. They dressed to be noticed, to gain approval, and to be fashionable.

Instead of being concerned about the oppression around them, they were self-serving and self-centered. Those who abuse their possessions will end up with nothing. These verses are not an indictment against clothing and jewelry, but a judgment on those who use them lavishly while blind to the needs of others. When God blesses you, don't flaunt it. Use what you have to help others.

CHECK IT OUT:

Proverbs 31:30. *Beauty doesn't last.*
Matthew 6:25-34. *Don't worry about clothing.*
1 Timothy 2:9-10. *Develop "inside appearance."*
1 Peter 3:3-5. *True beauty is a gentle and quiet spirit.*

ATTITUDES

Do Your Best

Bible Reading: Genesis 39:1-23

Key Verse: *The keeper of the prison did not look into anything that was under Joseph's authority, because the LORD was with him; and whatever he did, the LORD made it prosper.*
Genesis 39:23, NKJV

As a prisoner and slave, Joseph could have seen his situation as hopeless. Instead, he did his best with each small task given him. His diligence and positive attitude were soon noticed by the jail warden, who promoted him to prison administrator. Are you in the midst of a seemingly hopeless predicament? Whether at work, at home, or at school, follow Joseph's example by doing your best with each small task. Remember how God turned Joseph's situation around. He will see your efforts and can reverse even overwhelming odds.

Be Selfless

Bible Reading: Ruth 1:1-13

Key Verse: *And Naomi said to her two daughters-in-law, "Go, return each of you to her mother's house."* Ruth 1:8, NASB

There was almost nothing worse than being a widow in the ancient world. Widows were usually taken advantage of or ignored and were almost always poverty-stricken. God provided for the widow by requiring the nearest relative of her dead husband to care for her. But Naomi had no relatives in Moab, and she did not know if any of her relatives were alive in Israel.

In her desperate situation, Naomi had a very selfless attitude. She encouraged Ruth and Orpah to stay in Moab and start their lives over, even though this would mean hardship for herself. Like Naomi, we must consider the needs of others and not just our own. As Naomi discovered, when you reach out to others, they often reach back to you.

Listen to God

Bible Reading: 1 Samuel 1:12-17; 3:1-9

Key Verse: *So Eli told Samuel, "Go and lie down, and if he calls you, say, 'Speak, LORD, for your servant is listening.'" So Samuel went and lay down in his place.* 1 Samuel 3:9, NIV

Although this was the era when God still gave direct and audible messages to his people, such messages became rare in the days of Eli. Why? Look at the attitude of Eli's sons. They either refused to listen to God or allowed greed to get in the way of any communication with him.

Listening and responding are vital in a relationship with God. Although God may not use the sound of a human voice, he speaks just as clearly today through his Word, the Bible.

To receive his messages, we must be ready to listen and to act upon what he tells us. Like Samuel, be ready to say, "Here I am" and "Yes, I'm listening" when God calls you to action.

Keep Your Perspective

Bible Reading: 1 Samuel 17:1-51

Key Verse: *Moreover David said, "The LORD, who delivered me from*

*the paw of the lion and from the paw of the bear, He will
deliver me from the hand of this Philistine."*

1 Samuel 17:37, NKJV

What a difference perspective can make! Saul saw
only a giant and a young boy. David, however, saw a
mortal man defying almighty God. In addition, David
knew he would not be alone when he faced Goliath—
God would fight with him. David looked at his situation from God's perspective. Viewing impossible
situations from God's point of view helps us to put
giant problems in perspective.

Show Love and Respect

Bible Reading: 2 Kings 1:1-15

Key Verse: *So he again sent the captain of a third fifty with his fifty.
When the third captain of fifty went up, he came and
bowed down on his knees before Elijah, and begged him
and said to him, "O man of God, please let my life and
the lives of these fifty servants of yours be precious in
your sight."*

2 Kings 1:13, NASB

Notice how the third captain went to Elijah. Although
the first two captains called Elijah "man of God," they
were not being genuine. The third captain also called
him "man of God," but he humbly begged for mercy.
His attitude, which showed respect for God and his
power, saved the lives of his men. Effective living begins
with a right attitude toward God. Let respect charac-
terize your attitude toward God and others.

Leftovers

Bible Reading: Malachi 1:1-9

Key Verse: *"But now will you not entreat God's favor, that He may
be gracious to us? With such an offering on your part,
will He receive any of you kindly?" says the LORD of hosts.*

Malachi 1:9, NASB

God accused Israel of dishonoring him by offering
imperfect sacrifices. Unfortunately, we also have
offered imperfect sacrifices to God. Our lives should be

living sacrifices to God (Romans 12:1). If we give God only our leftover time, money, and energy, we repeat the same sin as these worshipers who didn't want to bring anything valuable to God. What we give God reflects our true attitude toward him.

How You Talk

Bible Reading: Acts 15:13-31

Key Verse: *Then the apostles and elders, with the whole church, decided to choose some of their own men and send them to Antioch with Paul and Barnabas.*   Acts 15:22, NIV

The letter sent to the Gentile Christians in Antioch answered their questions and brought them great joy. This beautifully written letter appealed to the Holy Spirit's guidance and explained what should be done as though the readers already knew it. As this letter illustrates, effective communication is accomplished when people are careful not only in what they say, but also in *how* they say it. We may be correct in what we say, but we can lose our audience by the tone of our voice or by the attitude that comes across in our delivery.

A New Attitude

Bible Reading: Romans 12:1-21

Key Verse: *Do not conform any longer to the pattern of this world, but be transformed by the renewing of your mind. Then you will be able to test and approve what God's will is—his good, pleasing and perfect will.*   Romans 12:2, NIV

The behavior and customs of this world are usually selfish and corrupting, and many Christians wisely decide that much worldly behavior is off-limits for them. Our refusal to conform to the world, however, must go even deeper than our level of behavior and customs—it must be firmly founded in our minds. This verse is also translated, "Do not be conformed to this world, but be transformed by the renewing of your mind" (NKJV). It is possible to avoid most worldly customs and still be proud, covetous, selfish, stubborn, and arrogant. Only when our minds are renewed by the new attitude Christ gives us are we truly transformed. If our character is like Christ's, we can be sure our behavior will honor God.

CHECK IT OUT:

Exodus 14:11-14. *Trusting God in bad times will help you to have a positive attitude.*

Numbers 13:25–14:4. *Be optimistic.*

Numbers 16:41-45. *Negative attitudes make things worse.*

Proverbs 15:15. *Attitudes determine life.*

Obadiah 1:2-10. *A cocky attitude is dangerous to have.*

Jonah 3–4. *Misplaced priorities can leave you with a bad attitude.*

Habakkuk 3:17-19. *Have a good attitude in bad times.*

Matthew 5:3-12. *Be happy and blessed by obeying God.*

John 3:1-21. *Be willing to learn.*

Ephesians 4:23. *Your attitudes should be changing for the better.*

Philippians 2:5. *Your attitude should be the same one shown by Jesus.*

(see also Caring for Others, Christian Life, and Lifestyle)

AUTHORITY

Listen to Your Parents

Bible Reading: Numbers 30:1-16

Key Verse: *But if her father overrules her on the day that he hears, then none of her vows nor her agreements by which she has bound herself shall stand; and the LORD will release her, because her father overruled her.* Numbers 30:5, NKJV

Under Israelite law, parents could overrule their children's vows. This helped young people avoid making foolish promises or costly commitments. From this law comes an important principle for both parents and children. Young people still living at home should seek their parents' help when they make decisions. A parent's experience could save a child from a serious mistake. Parents, however, should exercise their authority with caution and grace. They should let children learn from their mistakes while protecting them from disaster.

Parents Have Good Advice

Bible Reading: Proverbs 6:1-23

Key Verse: *My son, keep your father's command, and do not forsake the law of your mother.* Proverbs 6:20, NKJV

It is natural and good for children, as they grow toward adulthood, to strive to become independent of their parents. Young adults, however, should take care not to turn a deaf ear to their parents—rejecting their parents' advice just when they may need it most. If you are struggling with a decision or looking for insight, check with your parents or other older, trustworthy adults who know you well. Their extra years of experience may have given them the wisdom you seek.

Show Respect for Authority

Bible Reading: 1 Samuel 24:1-22

Key Verse: *So he said to his men, "Far be it from me because of the LORD that I should do this thing to my lord, the LORD's anointed, to stretch out my hand against him, since he is the LORD's anointed."* 1 Samuel 24:6, NASB

David had great respect for Saul, even though Saul was trying to kill him. Although Saul was in a state of sin and rebellion against God, David still respected the position Saul held as God's anointed king. David knew he would one day be king, and he also knew it was not right to strike down the man God had placed on the throne. If he assassinated Saul, he would be setting a precedent for his own opponents to remove him someday.

Romans 13:1-7 teaches that God has placed the government and its leaders in power. We may not know why, but, like David, we are to respect the positions and roles of those to whom God has given authority. There is one exception, however. Because God is our highest authority, we should not allow a leader to force us to violate God's law.

God Is the Ultimate Authority

Bible Reading: 1 Chronicles 6:48-49; 13:1-13

Key Verse: *But Aaron and his descendants were the ones who presented offerings on the altar of burnt offering and on the altar of incense in connection with all that was done in the Most Holy Place, making atonement for Israel, in accordance with all that Moses the servant of God had commanded.* 1 Chronicles 6:49, NIV

Aaron and his descendants strictly followed the details of worship commanded by God through Moses. They did not choose only those commands they *wanted* to obey. Note what happened to Uzza when important details in handling the ark of the covenant were neglected. We should not obey God selectively, choosing those commands we will obey and those we will ignore. God's Word has authority over every aspect of our lives, not just certain areas.

Appeal to a Higher Authority

Bible Reading: Philemon 1:1-25

Key Verses: *For this reason, though I am bold enough in Christ to command you to do your duty, yet I would rather appeal to you on the basis of love.* Philemon 1:8-9, NRSV

Because Paul was an apostle, he could have used his authority over Philemon to command him to deal kindly with his runaway slave. But Paul based his request not on his own authority, but on Philemon's Christian commitment. Paul wanted Philemon's heart-felt—not grudging—obedience. When you know something is right and you have the power to demand it, do you appeal to your authority or the other person's commitment? Here Paul provides a good example of how to deal with a possible conflict between Christian friends.

CHECK IT OUT:

Exodus 20:12; Deuteronomy 5:16. *Honor your parents.*

Judges 21:20-25. *Being your own authority invites disaster.*

Esther 10:3. *Use authority well.*

Proverbs 1:8-9. *Listen to your mother and father.*

Proverbs 13:24. *Parents should discipline their children.*

Proverbs 15:5. *Only a fool ignores his father's discipline.*

Proverbs 21:1. *God is the authorities' authority.*

Matthew 9:6. *God gave Jesus authority.*

Acts 4:7-12. *Jesus is our authority.*

Romans 13:1-7. *Obey the authorities.*

1 Corinthians 11:3, 11-12. *Husbands are the authority in marriage.*

Ephesians 6:1-3; Colossians 3:20. *Obey your parents.*

1 Thessalonians 5:12-13. *Honor church authorities.*

BELIEF

What Does God Expect of Me?

Bible Reading: Deuteronomy 10:12-22

Key Verses: *And now, O Israel, what does the LORD your God ask of you but to fear the LORD your God, to walk in all his ways, to love him, to serve the LORD your God with all your heart and with all your soul, and to observe the LORD's commands and decrees that I am giving you today for your own good?* Deuteronomy 10:12-13, NIV

Often we ask, "What does God expect of me?" Here Moses gives a summary that is simple in form and easy to remember. Here are the essentials: (1) Listen carefully to what God says. (2) Obey his commands. (3) Love and worship him with all your heart. How often we complicate faith with man-made rules, regulations, and requirements. Are you frustrated and burned-out from trying hard to please God? Concentrate on his real requirements—to respect, follow, and love him—and find peace.

Why Should I Believe in God?

Bible Reading: 1 Samuel 2:1-10

Key Verse: *No one is holy like the LORD, for there is none besides You, nor is there any rock like our God.* 1 Samuel 2:2, NKJV

Hannah praised God for being a Rock—firm, strong, and unchanging. In our fast-paced world, friends come and go, and circumstances change. It's difficult to find a solid foundation that will not change. Those who devote their lives to people, causes, or possessions are trusting in things that will pass away. But God will never pass away, even when everything else seems to be falling apart. Like Hannah, place your trust in him.

Put God in First Place

Bible Reading: 2 Kings 15:32-38; 2 Chronicles 27:1-9

Key Verses: *And he did what was right in the sight of the LORD. . . .
However the high places were not removed; the people
still sacrificed and burned incense on the high places.*
2 Kings 15:34-35, NKJV

"Jotham was a good king . . . *but.*" Much good can be
said of Jotham and his reign as king of Judah, but he
failed in a most critical area: He didn't destroy the
shrines to the false gods, although leaving them clearly
violated the first commandment (Exodus 20:3). Like
Jotham, we may live basically good lives and yet miss
doing what is most important. A lifetime of doing good
is not enough if we make the crucial mistake of not following God with all our hearts. A true follower of God
puts him first in all areas of life.

Get to Know God

Bible Reading: 2 Chronicles 6:12-21

Key Verse: *But will God indeed reside with mortals on earth? Even
heaven and the highest heaven cannot contain you, how
much less this house that I have built!*
2 Chronicles 6:18, NRSV

Solomon marveled that the temple could contain the
power of God and that God would be willing to live on
earth among sinful people. We marvel that God,
through his Son, Jesus, dwelt among us in human form
to reveal his eternal purposes to us. In doing so, God
was reaching out to mankind in love. God wants us to
reach out in return and get to know him. Only then will
we come to love him with all our hearts. Don't simply
marvel at his power; take time to get to know him.

Help with Daily Battles

Bible Reading: 2 Chronicles 20:1-19

Key Verse: *Thus says the LORD to you, "Do not fear or be dismayed
because of this great multitude, for the battle is not yours
but God's."* 2 Chronicles 20:15, NASB

As the enemy bore down on Judah, God spoke through Jahaziel: "Do not fear . . . for the battle is not yours but God's." We may not fight an enemy army, but every day we battle temptation, pressure, and "spiritual forces of evil in the heavenly places" (Ephesians 6:12, NRSV) who want us to rebel against God. We must remember that, as believers, we have God's Spirit in us. If we ask for God's help when we face struggles, God will fight for us—and God always triumphs.

How do we let God fight for us? (1) By realizing the battle is not ours, but God's; (2) by recognizing human limitations and allowing God's strength and power to work through our fears and weaknesses; (3) by making sure our battle is for God and not just our own selfish desires; and (4) by asking God for help in our daily battles.

Far beyond Our Understanding

Bible Reading: Job 36:26-33; 37:19-24

Key Verse: *Behold, God is great, and we do not know Him; nor can the number of His years be discovered.* Job 36:26, NKJV

One theme in the poetic literature of the Bible is that we cannot know God completely. This does not mean that we cannot have any knowledge about God, because the Bible is full of details about who he is, how we can know him, and how we can have an eternal relationship with him. What it means is that we can never know enough to predict his plans for our future or to manipulate God for our own ends. Life always has more questions than answers, and we must constantly go to God for fresh insights into life's dilemmas.

Only for Cowards?

Bible Reading: Psalm 18:6-35

Key Verse: *As for God, his way is perfect; the word of the LORD is flawless. He is a shield for all who take refuge in him.* Psalm 18:30, NIV

David was not a coward; he was a mighty warrior who, with all his armies and weapons, knew that only God could ultimately protect and save him. Many say belief in God is a crutch for weak people who cannot make it on their own. But those who say this don't realize that everyone is weak and in need of God. He is more than a crutch, though—he is a shield to protect us. He strengthens, protects, and guides us in order to send us back into an evil world to fight for him.

Show Reverence

Bible Reading: Psalms 86:1-17; 99:1-9

Key Verses: *The LORD is great in Zion; he is exalted over all the peoples. Let them praise your great and awesome name. Holy is he!* Psalm 99:2-3, NRSV

Everyone, even kings and rulers, should reverence God's great and holy name because his name symbolizes his nature, his personage, and his reputation. But the name of God is used so often in vulgar conversation that we have lost sight of its holiness. How easy it is to treat God lightly in everyday life. If you claim him as your father, live worthy of the family name. Reverence God's name by both your *words* and your *life.*

Reverencing God with your words means to be extremely careful how you use his name and how you speak. Reverencing God with your life means appreciating and honoring him in all areas of your life. If you reverence God with your whole heart, then your work, relationships, use of money, and desires will be in keeping with his will.

When You're Ridiculed for Your Faith

Bible Reading: Isaiah 51:1-11

Key Verse: *Listen to Me, you who know righteousness, you people in whose heart is My law: Do not fear the reproach of men, nor be afraid of their insults.* Isaiah 51:7, NKJV

Isaiah encouraged those who served God to discern right from wrong and to follow God's laws. He also gave them hope when they faced people's scorn or slander because of their faith. We need not fear when people ridicule us for our faith, because God is with us and truth will prevail. If people make fun of you or dislike you because you believe in God, remember that they are not against you personally but are against God. He will deal with them; you should concentrate on loving and obeying him.

CHECK IT OUT:

Exodus 20:2-7. *God must have first place in your life.*
2 Kings 5:13-15. *Belief leads to obedience.*
Psalm 14:1-4. *Only a fool says there is no God.*
Luke 12:8-9. *Jesus honors belief in him.*
John 1:12. *All who receive Christ become God's children.*
John 3:16. *God loved people so much that he sacrificed his own Son for them.*
John 12:37-43. *Popularity must not interfere with belief.*
2 Corinthians 5:7; 1 Peter 1:8. *Believe in what you cannot see.*
Acts 16:31; Romans 10:9-10. *Believe and be saved.*
Romans 1:18-25. *There is no excuse for unbelief.*
Romans 4:3; Galatians 3:6-9. *Belief in God makes us righteous.*

(see also Faith, God's Will, Salvation, and Trust)

BIBLE

The Bible and Science Class

Bible Reading: Genesis 1:1-31

Key Verse: *And God saw all that He had made, and behold, it was very good.* Genesis 1:31, NASB

Chances are the Bible's account of creation differs from what you hear in the typical high school science class. It may make you wonder who's right, why there's a difference, and how science and the Bible relate to one another.

It's important to remember that the Bible was not meant to be a science textbook. God's purpose in giving us the Bible was to let his creation know the most important things about life, about what to do in certain situations, and especially about the extent of his love for us. For some reason, he chose to leave out dinosaurs, fusion, and gravity (among other significant discoveries) and instead included stories about real people with real struggles and hardships. Some of those people conquered because they realized that God was with them. Others failed because they rejected God. The Bible tells us more about living a fulfilling life than we'll ever find in a science book. Above all, the Bible is the history of God's chosen people through whom Jesus Christ was born; it records Jesus' life on earth and the beginnings of Christianity.

In addition, the Bible gives us some basic truths about the origin and purpose of life that you won't get from a science book. First, the universe and all people were created by God. It takes more faith to believe that complex human beings materialized out of nothing than to believe that a loving and all-powerful God created us. And how much more fulfilling it is to realize that you have a purpose as a specific creation of God! Second, God created us in his own image. Exactly how he did that remains a matter of faith. But, if you struggle against the current teaching in your science class, take comfort in the knowledge of God's incredible love in creating the entire universe (including you) and calling it excellent in every way.

Don't, Don't, Don't

Bible Reading: Leviticus 19:1-18

Key Verse: *Do not seek revenge or bear a grudge against one of your people, but love your neighbor as yourself. I am the LORD.*
Leviticus 19:18, NIV

Don't, don't, don't. Some people think the Bible is nothing but a book of don'ts. But Jesus neatly summarized all these rules when he said to love God with all your heart and your neighbor as yourself. He called these the greatest commandments (or rules) of all (Matthew 22:34-40). By carrying out Jesus' simple commands, we find ourselves following all of God's other laws as well.

Get to Know What God Says

Bible Reading: 1 Chronicles 28:1-10

Key Verse: *Now . . . observe and search out all the commandments of the LORD your God; that you may possess this good land, and leave it for an inheritance to your children after you forever.*   1 Chronicles 28:8, NRSV

David told Solomon to search out and follow every one of God's commands to ensure Israel's prosperity and the continuation of David's descendants upon the throne. It was the solemn duty of the king to study and obey God's laws. The teachings of Scripture are the keys to security, happiness, and justice, but you'll never discover them unless you search God's Word. If God's will is ignored and his teaching neglected, anything we attempt to build, even if it has God's name on it, is headed for collapse. Get to know God's commands through regular Bible study, and obey them every day.

That Bible on the Shelf

Bible Reading: 2 Chronicles 34:14-33

Key Verse: *Then the king stood in his place and made a covenant before the LORD, to follow the LORD, and to keep His commandments and His testimonies and His statutes with all his heart and all his soul, to perform the words of the covenant that were written in this book.*

2 Chronicles 34:31, NKJV

When Josiah read the scroll that Hilkiah discovered, he responded with repentance and humility and promised to follow God's commandments as written on the scroll. The Bible is God's Word to us, full of living power (Hebrews 4:12), but we cannot know what God wants us to do if we do not read it. Even reading God's Word is not enough; we must be willing to do what it says. There is not much difference between the scroll hidden in the temple and the Bible hidden on the bookshelf. An unread Bible is just as useless as a lost scroll.

What's the Difference?

Bible Reading: Psalm 119:105-125

Key Verse: *I am your servant; give me discernment that I may understand your statutes.*   Psalm 119:125, NIV

Faith comes alive when we apply Scripture to our lives. With the psalmist, we need the common sense and the desire to apply God's Word to all areas of our lives—especially those where we need help. The Bible is like medicine—it goes to work only when you apply it to the infected areas of your life. As you read the Bible, be on the alert for lessons, commands, or examples that you can apply to your life.

God's Word Endures Forever

Bible Reading: Jeremiah 36:1-32

Key Verse: *Then the word of the LORD came to Jeremiah after the king had burned the scroll and the words which Baruch had written at the dictation of Jeremiah.* Jeremiah 36:27, NASB

God told Jeremiah to write his words on a scroll. Because he was not allowed to go to the temple, Jeremiah asked his scribe, Baruch, to whom he had dictated the scroll, to read it to the people gathered there. Baruch then read it to the officials, and finally Jehudi read it to the king himself. Although the king burned the scroll, he could not destroy God's Word. Today many people try to put God's Word aside or say that it contains errors and therefore cannot be trusted. People may reject God's Word, but they cannot destroy it. God's Word will stand forever (Psalm 119:89).

How to Have Devotions

Bible Reading: John 20:19-31

Key Verses: *And truly Jesus did many other signs in the presence of His disciples, which are not written in this book; but these are written that you may believe that Jesus is the Christ, the Son of God, and that believing you may have life in His name.*   John 20:30-31, NKJV

If you're just beginning to study the Bible or if you're a new Christian, you probably will not want to try to begin at Genesis and read straight through. The entire Bible is "useful to teach us," but some of it can be difficult reading until you understand some of the basics.

So, for now, consider these suggestions:

Your first priority is to get to know Jesus Christ, so begin with the Gospels. The four Gospels give different perspectives on Jesus' life. The Gospel of Mark is short and fast-paced, so you might want to start there. Listen to Jesus' words. Try to understand what each story is saying. Notice how Jesus treats people.

Next, read through some of the shorter letters that Paul, Peter, and John wrote (Paul's letters are everything from Romans through Philemon). Start with Philippians.

Try Proverbs next. You can read one chapter a day and finish the book in a month.

After this, read Genesis, Exodus, Daniel, and Jonah. They offer stories of real people whose problems were not all that different from yours. Learn from their lives so that you don't make the same mistakes they did.

There is no shortcut to the Christian life. We must be disciplined enough to dig into the Bible to find all the buried treasure that God wants to give those who will take the time to read and study. Have fun!

Let the Bible Be Your Guide

Bible Reading: 2 Corinthians 11:2-15

Key Verse: *But I am afraid . . . your minds should be led astray from the simplicity and purity of devotion to Christ.*

2 Corinthians 11:3, NASB

Some Corinthian believers fell for false teaching that sounded good and seemed to make sense. Unfortunately, there will always be people who twist the Good News. Either they do not understand what the Bible teaches, or they are uncomfortable with the truth as it is. That's why you shouldn't believe anyone simply because he or she sounds authoritative or says things you like to hear. But how can you tell when others are twisting the truth? You can do two things. First, find out what the group or person teaches about Jesus Christ. Second, check the group's or person's words against God's. If their teaching does not match the truth of God's Word, then it is twisted. Remember, the Bible should always be your authoritative guide to all teaching.

The Source

Bible Reading: 2 Timothy 3:1-17

Key Verse: *All scripture is inspired by God and is useful for teaching, for reproof, for correction, and for training in righteousness.* 2 Timothy 3:16, NRSV

The whole Bible is God's inspired Word. Because it is inspired and trustworthy, we should *read* it and *apply* it to our lives. The Bible is our standard for testing everything else that claims to be true. It is our safeguard against false teaching and our source of guidance for how we should live. The Bible is our only source of knowledge about how we can be saved. God wants to show you what is true and equip you to live for him. How much time do you spend in God's Word? Read it regularly to discover God's truth and to become confident in your life and faith. Develop a plan for reading the whole Bible, not just the same familiar passages.

CHECK IT OUT:

Psalm 119:18-20, 25, 97-104. *The Bible guides us, revives us, and gives us wisdom.*

Matthew 4:3-4. *Use Scripture to resist temptation.*

Colossians 2:6-7. *Gain nourishment in daily devotions.*

2 Timothy 2:15. *Handle God's Word with care.*

Hebrews 4:12. *God's Word is powerful.*

2 Peter 1:16-21. *The Bible contains accurate eyewitness accounts of Christ's life.*

1 John 2:12-17. *The Bible has practical advice.*

Revelation 22:18-19. *Don't change or add to the Bible.*

(see also God's Will and Obedience)

CARING FOR OTHERS

Foreign Exchange

Bible Reading: Exodus 22:21-31

Key Verse: *You shall neither mistreat a stranger nor oppress him, for you were strangers in the land of Egypt.*

Exodus 22:21, NKJV

God warned the Israelites not to treat strangers unfairly because they themselves were once strangers in Egypt. It is not easy coming to a new environment where you feel alone and out of place. Are there strangers in your corner of the world? new arrivals at school? immigrants from another country? Be sensitive to their struggles, and express God's love through kindness and generosity.

Offer Support to a Friend

Bible Reading: 1 Samuel 1:1-18

Key Verse: *And it happened year after year, as often as she went up to the house of the LORD, she would provoke her, so she wept and would not eat.* 1 Samuel 1:7, NASB

Part of God's plan for Hannah involved postponing her years of childbearing. While Peninnah and Elkanah looked at Hannah's outward circumstances, God was moving ahead with his plan. Can you think of others who are struggling with the way God is working in their lives and who need your support? By supporting those who are struggling, you may help them stay obedient to God and confident in his plan for their lives.

When a Friend Is Grieving

Bible Reading: Job 16:1-22

Key Verse: *But my mouth would encourage you; comfort from my lips would bring you relief.* Job 16:5, NIV

Job's friends were supposed to be comforting him in his grief. Instead, they condemned him for causing his own suffering. Job began his reply to Eliphaz by calling him and his friends "miserable comforters." Job's words reveal several ways to become a better comforter to those in pain: (1) Don't talk just for the sake of talking; (2) don't sermonize by giving pat answers; (3) don't criticize; (4) put yourself in the other person's place; and (5) offer help and encouragement. Often, we feel we must say something spiritual and insightful to a hurting friend. Perhaps what he or she needs most is just our presence to show that we care. Pat answers and trite quotations say much less than caring silence and loving companionship. Try Job's suggestions, knowing that they are given by a person who needed great comfort. The best comforters are those who know something about personal suffering.

How to Help the Needy

Bible Reading: Matthew 25:31-46

Key Verse: *The King will reply, "I tell you the truth, whatever you did for one of the least of these brothers of mine, you did for me."* Matthew 25:40, NIV

At the end of time, God will separate his obedient followers from pretenders and unbelievers. The real evidence of a person's belief will be the way he or she has acted. That is to say, what we do for others demonstrates what we really think about Jesus' words. How well do your actions separate you from pretenders and unbelievers? Do you feed the hungry, give the homeless a place to stay, or visit the sick?

Exercise a Servant Heart

Bible Reading: 1 Corinthians 10:29-33

Key Verse: *For I am not seeking my own good but the good of many, so that they may be saved.* 1 Corinthians 10:33, NIV

Paul was not concerned with what he liked best but with what was best for those around him. Unfortunately, not all Christians have servant attitudes and hearts like Paul's. Some are insensitive toward others and do what they want, no matter who is hurt by their actions. Others do the exact opposite and are oversensitive to people's feelings, doing nothing for fear someone may be displeased. Still some Christians are yes-men who are more concerned with gaining the approval of people rather than God. None of these attitudes come close to the intent of Paul's statement. What Paul meant is that we should make the welfare of others one of our primary goals in this "me-first," "look-out-for-number-one" age. When we do this, we begin to develop a servant's heart.

Words of Encouragement

Bible Reading: 1 Thessalonians 5:1-11

Key Verse: *Therefore encourage one another and build up each other, as indeed you are doing.*

1 Thessalonians 5:11, NRSV

As you near the end of a foot race, your legs ache, your throat burns, and your whole body cries out for you to stop. This is when friends and fans are most valuable. Their encouragement helps you push through the pain to the finish. In the same way, Christians are to encourage one another. A word of encouragement offered at the right moment can be the difference between finishing well and collapsing along the way. Look around you. Be sensitive to others' need for encouragement, and offer supportive words or actions.

CHECK IT OUT:

2 Kings 4:32-37. *God cares for the hurting and afflicted.*
Matthew 6:30. *God cares for you intimately.*
Matthew 8:14-15. *Serve others out of gratitude to Christ.*
Luke 10:29-37. *Jesus teaches about caring for others.*
John 11:32-44; 13:3-5. *Jesus is our example.*
Acts 20:28-35. *Caring causes others to care.*
Romans 1:6-9. *Let others know you care.*
1 Corinthians 9:19-23. *Paul shows how to care for others when witnessing.*

Philippians 2:5-8. *Serve as Jesus served.*
1 Timothy 5:4. *Christians should care for one another.*

CHOICES
(SEE DECISIONS)

CHRISTIAN LIFE

Growing Takes a Lifetime

Bible Reading: Deuteronomy 7:16-26

Key Verse: *But the LORD your God shall deliver them before you, and will throw them into great confusion until they are destroyed.* Deuteronomy 7:23, NASB

Moses told the Israelites that God would destroy Israel's enemies, but not all at once. God had the power to destroy those nations instantly, but he chose to do it in stages. In the same way and with the same power, God could miraculously and instantaneously change your life. Usually, however, he chooses to help you change gradually, teaching you one lesson at a time. Rather than expect instant spiritual maturity and solutions to all your problems, have realistic expectations and work on one problem at a time, trusting God to make up the difference between where you should be and where you are now. You'll soon look back and see that a miraculous transformation has occurred.

When You Face Hatred

Bible Reading: Psalm 74:1-23

Key Verse: *They said in their hearts, "Let us destroy them altogether." They have burned up all the meeting places of God in the land.* Psalm 74:8, NKJV

When enemy armies defeated Israel, they sacked Jerusalem, trying to wipe out every trace of God. This has often been the response of people who hate God.

Today many are trying to erase all traces of God from traditions in our society and subjects taught in our schools. Do what you can to help maintain a Christian influence, but don't become discouraged when others appear to make great strides in eliminating all traces of God, for they cannot eliminate his presence in the lives of believers.

Strength of Character

Bible Reading: Proverbs 31:10-31

Key Verses: *Her children rise up and call her happy; her husband too, and he praises her: "Many women have done excellently, but you surpass them all."*

Proverbs 31:28-29, NRSV

Proverbs has a lot to say about women. How fitting that the book ends with a picture of "the best of them all"— a woman of strong character, great wisdom, many skills, and great compassion.

Some people have the mistaken idea that the ideal woman in the Bible is retiring, servile, and entirely domestic. Not so! This woman is an excellent wife and mother. She is also a manufacturer, importer, manager, realtor, farmer, seamstress, upholsterer, and merchant. Her strength and dignity do not come from her amazing achievements, however. They are a result of her reverence for God.

In our society, where physical appearance counts for so much, it may surprise us to realize that her appearance is never mentioned. Her attractiveness comes entirely from her character.

Despite the woman's outstanding abilities, she may not be one woman at all—she may be a composite portrait of ideal womanhood. Therefore, do not see her as a model to imitate in every detail; your days are not long enough to do everything she did! See her instead as an inspiration to be all you can be. We can't be just like her, but we can learn from her industry, integrity, and resourcefulness.

Are You Trying to Please Everybody?

Bible Reading: Mark 15:1-15

Key Verse: *Wanting to satisfy the crowd, Pilate released Barabbas to them. He had Jesus flogged, and handed him over to be crucified.* Mark 15:15, NIV

Although Jesus was innocent according to Roman law, Pilate caved in under political pressure. He abandoned what he knew was right. He tried to second-guess the Jewish leaders and give a decision that would please everyone while keeping himself safe. When we lay aside God's clear statements of right and wrong and make decisions based on our audience, we fall into compromise and lawlessness. God promises to honor those who do right, not those who make everyone happy.

Glorify Christ

Bible Reading: Galatians 1:13-24

Key Verse: *And they were glorifying God because of me.* Galatians 1:24, NASB

Paul's changed life caused many comments from people who saw or heard of him. His new life astonished them, and they glorified God because only God could have turned this zealous persecutor of Christians into a Christian himself. When you became a Christian, you may not have had as dramatic a change as Paul had, but even so, your new life should glorify the Savior. When people look at you, do they recognize that God has made changes in you? If not, perhaps you are not living as you should.

Bear Fruit

Bible Reading: Galatians 5:16-26

Key Verses: *But the fruit of the Spirit is love, joy, peace, patience, kindness, goodness, faithfulness, gentleness, self-control; against such things there is no law.* Galatians 5:22-23, NASB

The Spirit produces character traits, not specific actions. We can't go out and *do* these things, and we can't obtain them by trying to *get* them. If we want the fruit of the Spirit to develop in our lives, we must recognize that all of these characteristics are found in Christ. Thus the way to grow them is to join our lives to his (see John 15:4-5). We must know Christ, love him, remember him, and imitate him. The result will be that we will fulfill the intended purpose of the Law—loving God and man. Which spiritual fruits need further development in your life?

When Progress Seems Slow

Bible Reading: Colossians 2:1-23

Key Verse: *And you have been given fullness in Christ, who is the head over every power and authority.*

Colossians 2:10, NIV

People should be able to see a difference between the way Christians and non-Christians live. Still, we should not expect new Christians to achieve instant maturity. The Christian life is a process. Although we have a new nature, we don't automatically have all good thoughts and attitudes when we become new people in Christ. But if we keep listening to God, we will be changing all the time. As you look over the last year, what changes for the better have you seen in your thoughts and attitudes? Change may be slow, but your life will change significantly if you trust God to change you.

CHECK IT OUT:

Leviticus 19:1-2. *You must be holy because God is holy.*
Proverbs 20:11. *How we act shows who we are.*
Matthew 6:1-4, 16-18. *Live God's way.*
Matthew 12:33-37. *Your words can show your character.*
Hebrews 12:1-4. *Run the race.*
James 1:21-27. *Act on God's Word.*

(see also Attitudes and Lifestyle)

CHURCH

The Five Ws of Worship

Bible Reading: Psalm 100

Key Verse: *For the LORD is good; His mercy is everlasting, and His truth endures to all generations.* Psalm 100:5, NKJV

Whom do we worship? We worship God—not ourselves, not our church, not even what God does for us. We worship God for who he is.

What is worship? Worship is giving God the glory and obedience he deserves. In a sense, our whole life should be worship, but we do need time in church to focus on worship.

When should we worship? We can worship anytime, anywhere, but the Bible does tell us to set aside certain regular times for worship. Most churches meet on Sunday mornings, Sunday nights, and Wednesday nights.

Where should we worship? Again, God hears our worship from anywhere, be it a church building, a school, a storefront, a home, a prison, a hospital, wherever. It's not the place, but the person worshiped (God), that is important.

Why should we worship? First, we worship because God wants us to. Second, we worship because we need to. When we bow before God and acknowledge his greatness, not only is he pleased, but it puts us into right relationship with him. So when you go to church on Sunday, put your heart into your worship. God is waiting to hear from you.

More Than Rituals

Bible Reading: Isaiah 58:1-14

Key Verses: *If you refrain from trampling the sabbath, from pursuing your own interests on my holy day; if you call the sabbath a delight and the holy day of the LORD honorable; if you honor it, not going your own ways, serving your own interests, or pursuing your own affairs; then you shall take delight in the LORD.* Isaiah 58:13-14, NRSV

True worship was more than religious ritual, going to the temple every day and listening to Scripture readings. These people missed the point of a living, vital relationship with God. He doesn't want fasting or pious actions when people perform sinful practices with their hands and have unforgiven sin in their hearts. Even more important than correct worship and doctrine is genuine compassion for the poor, the helpless, and the oppressed.

Wholehearted Worship

Bible Reading: Lamentations 2:1-7

Key Verse: *The Lord has rejected his altar and abandoned his sanctuary. He has handed over to the enemy the walls of her palaces; they have raised a shout in the house of the* LORD *as on the day of an appointed feast.*

Lamentations 2:7, NIV

Our place of worship is not so important to God as our pattern of worship. A church may be beautiful, but if its people don't sincerely follow God, it decays from within. The people of Judah, despite their beautiful temple, had rejected in their daily lives what they proclaimed by their worship rituals. Thus their worship turned into a mocking lie. When you worship, are you saying words you don't really mean? Do you pray for help you don't really believe will come? Do you express love for God you don't really have? Earnestly seek God, and catch a fresh vision of his love and care. Then worship him wholeheartedly.

New Life for Old Bones

Bible Reading: Ezekiel 37:1-14

Key Verse: *Thus says the Lord* GOD *to these bones, "Behold, I will cause breath to enter you that you may come to life."*

Ezekiel 37:5, NASB

The dry bones represented the people's spiritually dead condition. Your church may seem like a heap of dried-up bones to you, spiritually dead with no hope of vitality. But just as God promised to restore his nation, he can restore any church, no matter how dry or dead it may be. Rather than give up, pray for renewal, for God can restore it to life. The hope and prayer of every church should be that God will put his Spirit into it (37:14). In fact, God is at work calling his people back to himself, bringing new life into dead churches.

What Is the Church?

Bible Reading: Matthew 16:13-19

Key Verse: *And I also say to you that you are Peter, and on this rock I will build My church, and the gates of Hades shall not prevail against it.* Matthew 16:18, NKJV

What exactly is the church? It is the group of all believers all over the world—those who follow Jesus and proclaim him as Lord. Unfortunately, the church is often misunderstood. Some people think the church is nothing more than a building. While the places where believers meet are called churches, the real "church" is made of people—God's people. When we "go to church," we meet with God's people to worship and learn about God. So in a real sense, wherever Christians gather, there's a church.

Another misconception some people have about church is that church is just for good people or people pretending to be good (also called hypocrites). But the church isn't for "good" people; it's for sinners who know they've been forgiven and who come together regularly to celebrate God's love and mercy.

Finally, some people believe that churches are made up of the same kinds of people. But this simply isn't true. The early church had believers who were slaves, servants, Jews, Gentiles, men, women, old people, and young people. Today, churches contain many different people from all walks of life. How amazing that God loves and uses all these different people, bringing them together for the united purpose of worshiping and serving him. Statements of faith, styles of worship, location of worship, financial ability, focus of ministry—these differ from church to church. But with all those differences aside, we must remember that we are all part of one big family—God's family.

Even Jesus Went to Church

Bible Reading: Luke 4:14-22

Key Verse: *When he came to Nazareth, where he had been brought up, he went to the synagogue on the sabbath day, as was his custom.* Luke 4:16, NRSV

Jesus went to the synagogue "as usual." Even though he was the perfect Son of God, and his local synagogue left much to be desired, he attended services every week. Jesus' example makes most excuses for not attending church sound weak and self-serving. Make regular worship a part of your life.

We Need Other Believers

Bible Reading: Hebrews 10:15-25

Key Verse: *Not forsaking our own assembling together, as is the habit of some, but encouraging one another; and all the more, as you see the day drawing near.* Hebrews 10:25, NASB

To neglect Christian meetings is to give up the encouragement and help of other Christians. We gather together to share our faith and strengthen each other in the Lord. As we get closer to the time of Christ's return, anti-Christian forces will grow in strength, and we may face many spiritual struggles, tribulations, and even persecution. Difficulties, however, should never be excuses for missing church services. Rather, as difficulties arise, we should make an even greater effort to be faithful in attendance.

CHECK IT OUT:

Malachi 1:6-14. *God hates worthless worship and halfhearted devotion.*

John 4:21-24. *Worship is very important.*

Acts 2:42-47. *The believers praised God and obeyed his commandments.*

Romans 12:4-21. *The church is the body of Christ.*

Ephesians 5:19. *Make music in your heart to the Lord.*

COMMITMENT

How Strong Is My Commitment?

Bible Reading: Genesis 22:1-14

Key Verse: *"Do not lay a hand on the boy," he said. "Do not do anything to him. Now I know that you fear God, because you have not withheld from me your son, your only son."*
Genesis 22:12, NIV

God gave Abraham a test, not to make him stumble, but to deepen his capacity to obey God and thus to develop his character. God did not want Isaac to die, but he wanted Abraham to prove that he loved God more than he loved his promised and long-awaited son. Through this difficult experience, Abraham's commitment to obey God was strengthened. He also learned about God's ability to provide. The purpose of testing is to strengthen our character, to deepen our commitment to God, and to trust his perfect timing. Just as fire refines ore to extract precious metals, God refines us through difficult circumstances. When we are tested we can complain, or we can try to see how God is stretching us to develop our character.

Be Bold

Bible Reading: Ezra 5:1–6:15

Key Verse: *This was their reply to us: "We are the servants of the God of heaven and earth, and we are rebuilding the house that was built many years ago, which a great king of Israel built and finished."* Ezra 5:11, NRSV

While rebuilding the temple, the workers were confronted by the governor, demanding to know who gave permission for their construction project. This could have been intimidating, but, as we learn from the letter, they boldly replied, "We are the servants of the God of heaven and earth."

It is not always easy to speak up for our faith in an unbelieving world, but we must. The way to deal with pressure and intimidation is to recognize that we work for God. Our allegiance is to God first, people second. When we contemplate the reactions and criticisms of hostile people, we can become paralyzed with fear. If we make a policy of offending no one or pleasing everyone, our service to God will lose its effectiveness. God is our leader, and his rewards are most important. So don't be intimidated. Let others know by your actions and words whom you serve.

When the Going Gets Tough

Bible Reading: Matthew 8:14-27

Key Verse: *Jesus replied, "Foxes have holes and birds of the air have nests, but the Son of Man has no place to lay his head."*
Matthew 8:20, NIV

Following Jesus is not always an easy or comfortable road to travel. Often it means great cost and sacrifice, with no earthly rewards or security. Jesus didn't have a place to call home. You may find that following Christ costs you popularity, friendships, leisure time, or treasured habits. But while the costs of following Christ are high, the value of being Christ's disciple is an investment that lasts for eternity and yields incredible rewards.

Jesus' disciples knew this was true. Peter and the other disciples paid a high price—leaving their homes and jobs—to follow Jesus (see Luke 18:26-30). But Jesus reminded Peter that following him has its benefits as well as its sacrifices. Any believer who has had to give up something to follow Christ will be paid back in this life, as well as in the next. For example, if you must give up friends, you will find that God offers a secure relationship with himself now and forever. If you must give up your family's approval, you will gain the love of the family of God. The disciples had begun to pay the price of following Jesus, and Jesus said they would be rewarded. Don't dwell on what you have given up. Instead, think about what you have gained, and give thanks for it. You can never outgive God.

The Cost of Commitment

Bible Reading: Mark 9:35-50

Key Verse: *And if your eye causes you to sin, pluck it out. It is better for you to enter the kingdom of God with one eye than to have two eyes and be thrown into hell.*

Mark 9:47, NIV

Jesus used startling language to stress the importance of cutting sin out of our lives. Painful discipline is required of his true followers. Giving up a relationship, job, or habit that is against God's will may seem just as painful as cutting off a hand. Spending eternity in Christ's presence, however, is worth any sacrifice. Therefore, we must be ruthless in removing sins from our lives now in order to avoid being stuck with them for eternity. Nothing should stand in the way of faith. Make your choices from an eternal perspective.

Give It All to God

Bible Reading: Romans 12:1-11

Key Verse: *I appeal to you therefore . . . to present your bodies as a living sacrifice, holy and acceptable to God, which is your spiritual worship.*

Romans 12:1, NRSV

How much does God want? To put it bluntly, he wants everything. He doesn't want to be just "another part" of your life, along with work and friends and sports. Think of your life as a bicycle tire. The spokes are all the parts of your life, but the hub of the wheel is what holds everything together and keeps the wheel in balance. God wants to be the "hub" of your life, the central focus around which everything else in your life revolves. This means that he goes with you to all your activities. He's with you through the good times and rough times, and he should be the first one you turn to with your needs, problems, and praise. By keeping God at the center of your life and activities, he'll be in charge and you'll stay in balance. Don't let anything else take God's place in your life.

CHECK IT OUT:

> Ruth 1:1-19. *Ruth exhibited a true commitment to her friend Naomi.*
> Psalm 37:1-11. *Commit all you do to the Lord.*
> Matthew 10:32-33. *Be committed to Christ.*
> Matthew 13:18-23. *Be committed to Christ, even in tough times.*
> Luke 14:25-31. *It takes discipline to stay committed.*
> John 1:49. *Nathanael shows his commitment to Christ.*
> Acts 24:16. *Commit yourself, like Paul, to live right.*

COMPLAINING

Why Are You Complaining?

Bible Reading: Numbers 21:1-15

Key Verse: *And the people spoke against God and Moses, "Why have you brought us up out of Egypt to die in the wilderness? For there is no food and no water, and we loathe this miserable food."* Numbers 21:5, NASB

In Psalm 78 we learn the reasons behind Israel's complaining: (1) They forgot the miracles God did for them, (2) they demanded more than what God had given them, (3) their repentance was insincere, and (4) they were ungrateful for what God had done for them. Our complaining often has its roots in one of these thoughtless actions and attitudes. But we can keep complaining from taking hold in our lives by cutting it off at the source. The next time you complain, identify your reason for doing so. Then take the action necessary to remedy the real problem.

Complaining or Changing?

Bible Reading: 1 Samuel 7:1-17

Key Verse: *Then Samuel spoke to all the house of Israel, saying, "If you return to the LORD with all your hearts, then put away the foreign gods and the Ashtoreths from among you, and prepare your hearts for the LORD, and serve*

Him only; and He will deliver you from the hand of the Philistines."   1 Samuel 7:3, NKJV

Sorrow gripped Israel for twenty years. The ark was put away like an unwanted box in an attic, and it seemed as if the Lord had abandoned his people. Samuel, now a grown man, roused them to action by saying that if they were truly sorry, they should do something about it. How easy it is for us to complain about our problems, even to God, while we refuse to act, to change, and to do what he requires. Sadly, we don't even obey the commands he has already given us in his Word. Do you ever feel as if God has abandoned you? Check to see if there is anything he has already told you to do. You may not be able to receive new guidance until you have acted on his previous directions.

When You Just Want Answers

Bible Reading: Job 40:1-24

Key Verse: *Shall a faultfinder contend with the Almighty? Anyone who argues with God must respond.*   Job 40:2, NRSV

How do you argue with almighty God? Do you demand answers when things don't go your way, you get cut from a team, someone close to you is ill or dies, money is tight, you fail, or unexpected changes occur? The next time you are tempted to complain to God, consider how much he loves you, and remember Job's reaction when he had his chance to speak. Are you worse off than Job, or more righteous? Give God a chance to reveal his greater purposes for you, but remember that they may unfold over the course of your life and not at any given moment.

What Might God Be Saying?

Bible Reading: Acts 8:1-17

Key Verse: *Those who had been scattered preached the word wherever they went.*   Acts 8:4, NIV

Persecution forced the believers out of their homes in Jerusalem, but with them went the gospel. Often we have to become uncomfortable before we'll move. Discomfort may be unwanted, but it is not undesirable, for out of our hurting, God works his purposes. The next time you are tempted to complain about uncomfortable or painful circumstances, stop and ask if God may be preparing you for a special task.

An Opportunity in Disguise

Bible Reading: Acts 25:7-27

Key Verse: *And so, on the next day when Agrippa had come together with Bernice . . . and had entered the auditorium accompanied by the commanders and the prominent men of the city, . . . Paul was brought in.* Acts 25:23, NASB

Paul was in prison, but that didn't stop him from making the most of his situation. Military officers and prominent city leaders met in the palace with Agrippa to hear this case. Paul saw this new audience as yet another opportunity to present the gospel. Rather than complain about your present situation, look for opportunities to serve God and share him with others. Problems may be opportunities in disguise.

CHECK IT OUT:

Exodus 14:11-12. *Complaining hurts our faith in God.*
Psalm 39:1-7. *Take your complaints to God.*
Habakkuk 2:1. *Patiently wait for God's answer to your complaints.*
Philippians 2:14-16. *Do everything without complaining.*

CONFESSION

Take Responsibility

Bible Reading: 1 Chronicles 21:1-30

Key Verse: *David said to God, "I have sinned greatly in that I have done this thing. But now, I pray you, take away the guilt of your servant; for I have done very foolishly."*
1 Chronicles 21:8, NRSV

When David realized his sin, he took full responsibility, admitted he was wrong, and asked God to forgive him. Many people want to add God and his blessings to their lives without acknowledging their personal sin and guilt. But confession and repentance must come before receiving forgiveness. Like David, we must take full responsibility for our actions and confess them to God before we can expect him to forgive us and continue his work in our lives.

Come Back to God

Bible Reading: 2 Chronicles 6:14-31

Key Verse: *Then hear from heaven Your dwelling place, and forgive, and give to everyone according to all his ways, whose heart You know (for You alone know the hearts of the sons of men).* 2 Chronicles 6:30, NKJV

Have you ever felt far from God, separated by feelings of failure and personal problems? In his prayer, Solomon underscores the fact that God stands ready to hear us, to forgive our sins, and to restore our relationship with him. God is waiting and listening for our confessions of guilt and commitment to obey him. He is ready to forgive us and to restore us to fellowship with him. Don't wait to experience his loving forgiveness.

Confession Must Lead to Change

Bible Reading: Ezra 10:1-14

Key Verse: *Rise up; this matter is in your hands. We will support you, so take courage and do it.* Ezra 10:4, NIV

Following Ezra's earnest prayer, the people admitted their sin to God. Then they asked for direction in restoring their relationship with God. True repentance does not end with words of confession—that would be mere lip service. It must lead to corrected behavior and changed attitudes. When you sin and are truly sorry, confess this to God, ask his forgiveness, and accept his grace and mercy. Then, as an act of thankfulness for your forgiveness, change your ways.

No Sin Too Small

Bible Reading: Jeremiah 3:1-11

Key Verses: *Have you not just called to me: "My Father, my friend from my youth, will you always be angry? Will your wrath continue forever?" This is how you talk, but you do all the evil you can.* Jeremiah 3:4-5, NIV

Notice how the people of Israel minimized their sin. When we know we've done something wrong, we want to downplay the error by saying, "It wasn't that bad!" thereby relieving some of the guilt we feel. As we minimize our sinfulness, we naturally shy away from making changes, and so we keep on sinning. But if we view every wrong attitude and action as a serious offense against God, we will begin to understand what living for God is all about. Is there any sin in your life that you've written off as too small to worry about? God says that we must confess every sin and, having confessed it, turn from it.

CHECK IT OUT:

Psalm 32:5-6. *We must confess our sins.*

Psalm 51. *David's prayer of confession is a good example to follow.*

Psalm 66:16-20. *God listens when we confess.*

Luke 3:4-18. *John preached repentance plus good works.*

James 5:16. *We should confess to other believers.*

1 John 1:8-10. *God forgives when we confess.*

(see also Forgiveness and Repentance)

CONFORMITY
(SEE PEER PRESSURE)

CONSCIENCE

Yours Can Be Clear

Bible Reading: Job 27:1-7

Key Verse: *I will maintain my righteousness and never let go of it; my conscience will not reproach me as long as I live.*

Job 27:6, NIV

To all the accusations, Job was able to declare, "My conscience is clear." Only right living before God can bring a clear conscience, and how important Job's record became as he was being accused. Like Job, we can't claim sinless lives, but we *can* claim forgiven lives. When we confess our sins to God, we are forgiven and can live our lives with clear consciences (1 John 1:9).

Don't Let Yours Become Seared

Bible Reading: Hosea 5:1-9

Key Verse: *Their deeds do not permit them to return to their God. A spirit of prostitution is in their heart; they do not acknowledge the LORD.* Hosea 5:4, NIV

Persistent sin hardens a person's heart and makes it difficult to repent. Deliberately choosing to disobey God can sear the conscience; each sin makes the next one easier to commit. Don't allow sin to harden your heart. Steer as far away from sinful practices as possible.

Let Others Follow Theirs

Bible Reading: Romans 14:17–15:6

Key Verse: *But those who have doubts are condemned if they eat, because they do not act from faith; for whatever does not proceed from faith is sin.* Romans 14:23, NRSV

We try to steer clear of actions forbidden by Scripture, of course. But when Scripture is silent, we should follow our conscience. When God shows us something is wrong for us, we should avoid it. But we should not look down on other Christians who exercise their freedom in those areas.

Those Inner Tugs

Bible Reading: 1 Timothy 1:15-20

Key Verse: *This charge I commit to you, . . . that by [it] you may*

*wage the good warfare, having faith and a good
conscience, which some having rejected, concerning the
faith have suffered shipwreck, of whom are Hymenaeus
and Alexander, whom I delivered to Satan that they may
learn not to blaspheme.* 1 Timothy 1:18-19, NKJV

How can you keep your conscience clear? Treasure your
faith in Christ more than anything else, and do what
you know is right. Each time you deliberately ignore
your conscience, you are hardening your heart. Soon
your capacity to tell right from wrong will disappear.
But when you walk with God, he is able to speak to you
through your conscience, letting you know the difference between right and wrong. Be sure to act on those
inner tugs to do what is right—then your conscience
will remain clear.

CHECK IT OUT:

1 Samuel 24:1-8; 2 Samuel 24:10. *David listened to his conscience.*
Proverbs 3:1. *Follow God's instructions.*
Proverbs 20:27. *Our conscience is God's searchlight.*
Acts 24:16. *Paul talks about keeping a clear conscience.*
Romans 14:23. *Follow your conscience.*
1 Corinthians 4:4. *The Lord will examine us.*
1 Corinthians 9:25. *Deny yourself evil things.*
2 Timothy 2:1-7. *Do what your faith tells you.*

CONSEQUENCES OF SIN

Short-term Pleasure vs.
Long-term Consequences

Bible Reading: Genesis 25:27-34

Key Verse: *And Esau said, "Behold, I am about to die; so of what use
then is the birthright to me?"* Genesis 25:32, NASB

Esau traded the lasting benefits of his birthright for the
immediate pleasure of food. He acted on impulse, satis-
fying his immediate desires without pausing to consider the long-range consequences of what he was
about to do. We can fall into the same trap. When we

see something we want, our first impulse is to get it. At first we feel intensely satisfied and sometimes even powerful because we have obtained what we set out to get. But immediate pleasure often loses sight of the future.

Esau exaggerated his hunger. "I'm dying of starvation," he said. This thought made his choice much easier, because if he was starving, what good was an inheritance anyway? The pressure of the moment distorted his perspective and made his decision seem urgent. We often experience similar pressures. For example, when we feel sexual pressure, a marriage vow may seem unimportant. We sometimes feel such great pressure in one area that nothing else seems to matter, and we lose our perspective. Getting through that short, pressure-filled moment is often the hardest part of overcoming a temptation. We can avoid making Esau's mistake by comparing the short-term satisfaction with its long-range consequences before we act.

Consequences May Not Come Immediately

Bible Reading: Genesis 35:21-22; 49:1-4

Key Verse: *Turbulent as the waters, you will no longer excel, for you went up onto your father's bed, onto my couch and defiled it.* Genesis 49:4, NIV

As the oldest son, Reuben stood to receive a double portion of the family inheritance and a place of leadership among his people. But the consequences of his sin stripped away his rights and privileges and ruined his family. Reuben may have thought that he had gotten away with his sin, but his father, Jacob, remembered. On his deathbed, Jacob took away Reuben's double portion and gave it to another.

When we do something wrong, we may think, like Reuben, that we can escape unnoticed. But sin's consequences can plague us long after we have committed the act. The real consequences of sin are ruined lives. Before you give in to temptation, take a close look at the disastrous consequences that sin may have in your life and the lives of others. Then resist or flee, if necessary.

Why God Gives Rules

Bible Reading: Leviticus 20:22-27

Key Verse: *You are therefore to keep all My statutes and all My ordinances and do them, so that the land to which I am bringing you to live will not spew you out.*

Leviticus 20:22, NASB

God gave many rules to his people—but not without good reason. He did not withhold good from them; he only prohibited those acts that would bring them to ruin. All of us understand God's physical laws of nature. For example, jumping off a ten-story building means death because of the law of gravity. But some of us don't understand how God's spiritual laws work. God forbids us to do certain things because he wants to keep us from self-destruction. Next time you feel like doing something that you know is wrong, remember that the consequences might be suffering and separation from the God who loves you and is trying to help you.

Consequences Cannot Be Escaped

Bible Reading: 2 Chronicles 21:1-15

Key Verse: *He had also built high places on the hills of Judah and had caused the people of Jerusalem to prostitute themselves and had led Judah astray.*

2 Chronicles 21:11, NIV

Jehoram's reign was marked by sin and cruelty. He married a woman who worshiped idols. He killed his six brothers. He allowed and even promoted idol worship. Yet he was not killed in battle or by treachery—he died by a lingering and painful disease. Just because the punishment we may receive is not immediate or dramatic does not mean God is indifferent to our sin. We cannot ignore God's laws and think we are immune from the consequences of our sin. There can be no healing or deliverance for those who rebel against God until that relationship with God is made right.

CHECK IT OUT:

> Genesis 3:14-19. *Sin has consequences.*
> Exodus 34:7. *Consequences of sin are passed on.*
> Leviticus 26:14-33. *Disobedience brings consequences.*
> Deuteronomy 27:15-26. *God warns us of consequences.*
> 2 Samuel 11:1–12:18. *The consequences of David's sin were devastating.*
> 1 Chronicles 21:13-14. *Consider the consequences.*
> Matthew 10:32-33. *The consequences of denying Christ are serious.*
> 2 Corinthians 5:10. *Each of us will stand before God.*
> Galatians 6:7-9. *We will reap what we sow.*

CONTENTMENT

Bitter or Better?

Bible Reading: Genesis 33:1-20

Key Verse: *But Esau ran to meet him, and embraced him, and fell on his neck and kissed him, and they wept.*

Genesis 33:4, NKJV

It is refreshing to see Esau's change of heart when the two brothers meet again. The bitterness over losing his birthright and blessing (25:29-34) is gone. Instead, Esau is content with what he has. Jacob even exclaims how great it is to see his brother obviously pleased with him.

Life can deal us some bad situations. We can feel cheated, as Esau did, but we don't have to remain bitter. We can remove bitterness from our lives by honestly expressing our feelings to God, forgiving those who have wronged us, and being content with what we have.

Content in Going God's Way

Bible Reading: Psalm 23:1-6

Key Verse: *The LORD is my shepherd, I shall not be in want.*

Psalm 23:1, NIV

When we allow God our Shepherd to guide us, we will have contentment. When we choose to sin, however, we are choosing to go our own way, and we cannot blame God for the circumstances in which we find ourselves. Our Shepherd knows the meadow grass and quiet streams that will restore us. We will reach these places only by following him obediently. Rebelling against the Shepherd's leading is actually rebelling against our own best interests for the future. We must remember this the next time we are tempted to go our own way rather than the Shepherd's way.

Do I Need It or Just Want It?

Bible Reading: Psalm 34:1-22

Key Verse: *Fear the LORD, you his saints, for those who fear him lack nothing.* Psalm 34:9, NIV

"Those of us who reverence the Lord will never lack any good thing." At first we may question the truth of this statement because we lack many "good" things. This is not a blanket promise that all Christians will be rich. Instead, this is David's observation of God's goodness— all those who call upon God in their need will be answered, sometimes in unexpected ways.

Remember, our deepest needs are spiritual. While many Christians have more than enough possessions, many others face unbearable poverty and hardship. David was saying that to have God is to have all that a person needs. God is enough.

If you feel that you don't have everything you need, ask yourself these three questions: (1) Is this really a need? (2) Is this really good for me? (3) Is this the best time for me to have what I desire? Even if you answer yes to all three questions, God may allow you to go without it to help you grow more dependent on him. We may need to learn that we need *him* more than things.

Who's on First?

Bible Reading: Acts 20:18-38

Key Verse: *I have coveted no one's silver or gold or clothes.*
Acts 20:33, NASB

Paul was satisfied with whatever he had, wherever he was, as long as he could do God's work. Examine your attitudes toward wealth and comfort. If you focus more on what you don't have than on what you do have, it's time to reexamine your priorities and put God's work back in first place.

CHECK IT OUT:

Genesis 3:1-10. *Satan tries to ruin contentment.*
Psalm 17:13-15. *Contentment is not found in money or material things.*
Psalm 131:1-3. *Humility brings contentment.*
Matthew 6:25-35. *Be content with what you have.*
John 1:29-34. *Contentment comes when you put Jesus first.*
Philippians 4:10-14. *Be content in every situation.*
Hebrews 13:5-6. *Be content because God will never leave you.*

CRITICISM

When You're Criticized for Your Faith

Bible Reading: Psalm 79:1-13

Key Verse: *Why should the nations say, "Where is their God?" Let the avenging of the outpoured blood of your servants be known among the nations before our eyes.*

Psalm 79:10, NRSV

For reasons that we do not know, the heathen are allowed to scoff at believers. We should be prepared for criticism, jokes, and unkind remarks, because God does not place us beyond the attacks of scoffers. Therefore, we must endure suffering with patience and allow God to purify us through it.

If you face jealous critics because of your faith, be glad they're criticizing that part of your life—perhaps they had to focus on your religion as a last resort! Respond by continuing to believe in God, and live as you should. Then remember that God is in control, fighting this battle for you. In the end, God will bring himself glory (Psalm 76:10).

Sometimes the Truth Stings

Bible Reading: Jeremiah 19:14–20:6

Key Verses: *When the priest Pashhur son of Immer, the chief officer in the temple of the LORD, heard Jeremiah prophesying these things, he had Jeremiah the prophet beaten and put in the stocks at the Upper Gate of Benjamin at the LORD's temple.*

Jeremiah 20:1-2, NIV

Pashhur heard Jeremiah's words and, because of his guilt, locked Jeremiah up instead of taking his message to heart and acting upon it. The truth sometimes stings, but our reaction to the truth shows what we are made of. We can deny the charges and destroy evidence of our misdeeds, or we can take the truth humbly to heart and let it change us. Pashhur may have thought he was a strong leader, but he was really a coward.

Always Listen to God

Bible Reading: Jeremiah 28:1-17

Key Verses: *Then Jeremiah the prophet said to Hananiah the prophet, "Listen now, Hananiah, the LORD has not sent you, and you have made this people trust in a lie. "Therefore thus says the LORD, 'Behold, I am about to remove you from the face of the earth. This year you are going to die, because you have counseled rebellion against the LORD.'"*

Jeremiah 28:15-16, NASB

Jeremiah spoke the truth, even though it was unpopular. Hananiah spoke lies, and his deceitful words brought false hope and comfort to the people. Before their time, God had outlined the marks of a true prophet: A true prophet's predictions always come true, and his words never contradict previous revelation (Deuteronomy 13; 18:9-22). Jeremiah's predictions were already coming true, from Hananiah's death to the Babylonian invasions. But the people still preferred to listen to comforting lies rather than painful truth. Do your best to be open to God's words to you, even if you don't particularly like what he has to say. As painful as it may sometimes be, the truth is always best.

Be Less Critical of Others

Bible Reading: Luke 6:39-49

Key Verse: *And why do you look at the speck that is in your brother's eye, but do not notice the log that is in your own eye?*
Luke 6:41, NASB

Jesus doesn't mean we should ignore wrongdoing, but we are not to be so worried about others' sins that we overlook our own. We often rationalize our sins by pointing out the same mistakes in others. What kinds of specks in others' eyes are the easiest for you to criticize? Remember your own logs when you feel like criticizing, and you may find you have less to say.

How to Respond to Constructive Criticism

Bible Reading: Acts 8:14-24

Key Verse: *Simon answered, "Pray for me to the Lord, that nothing of what you have said may happen to me."* Acts 8:24, NRSV

Do you remember the last time a parent or friend strongly criticized you? Were you hurt? angry? defensive? Learn a lesson from Simon and his reaction to Peter's words. Simon exclaimed, "Pray for me!" When you are rebuked for a serious mistake, it is for your good. Admit your error and ask for prayer.

Destructive Criticism

Bible Reading: Galatians 5:13-26

Key Verse: *If you keep on biting and devouring each other, watch out or you will be destroyed by each other.*
Galatians 5:15, NIV

When we are not motivated by love, we become critical of others. We stop looking for good in them and see only their faults. Soon the unity of believers becomes broken. Have you talked behind someone's back? Have you focused on others' shortcomings instead of their strengths? Remind yourself of Jesus' command to love others as we love ourselves (Matthew 22:39). When you begin to feel critical of someone, make a list of that person's positive qualities. And don't say anything behind his or her back that you wouldn't say to that person's face.

CHECK IT OUT:

1 Samuel 1:6-10. *Don't let unjust criticism depress you.*

Psalm 141:5. *Accept helpful criticism.*

Proverbs 9:7-9. *Learn from criticism.*

Proverbs 13:18. *Honor can come from listening to the right criticism.*

Ecclesiastes 7:5. *Gladly receive criticism from a wise person.*

Matthew 7:1-6. *Change your own life; don't judge others.*

Titus 2:8. *Let your words be above criticism.*

1 Peter 3:16. *Live above criticism.*

DATING

Minor Differences?

Bible Reading: 1 Kings 3:1; 11:1-13

Key Verse: *Solomon did evil in the sight of the LORD, and did not fully follow the LORD, as did his father David.*

1 Kings 11:6, NKJV

Marriage between royal families was a common practice in the ancient Near East because it secured peace. Although Solomon's marital alliances built friendships with surrounding nations, they were also the beginning of his downfall. These relationships became inroads for pagan ideas and practices. Solomon's foreign wives brought their idols to Jerusalem and eventually lured him into idolatry.

It is easy to minimize religious differences in order to encourage the development of a friendship, but seemingly small differences can have an enormous impact upon a relationship. Christian/non-Christian dating relationships can sometimes lead to the non-Christian accepting Jesus, but it's very rare. Usually the Christian gets brought down by those who don't share his or her beliefs and values. God gives us standards to follow for all our relationships, including dating. If we follow God's will, we will not be lured away from our true focus.

Looking for Perfection?

Bible Reading: Proverbs 31:10-31

Key Verse: *Charm is deceptive, and beauty is fleeting; but a woman who fears the LORD is to be praised.* Proverbs 31:30, NIV

While this passage gives a picture of what a truly godly woman is like, it could also apply to a godly man. Note the key verse: Charm is deceptive and beauty doesn't last. So what does that mean for your dating life?

Quite simply, it means that you should look for more in a person than just physical appearance. While looks are important, they must not be all-important. Everyone ought to try to look his or her best, be clean and neat, etc. But beyond that, everyone looks different, and we should appreciate our uniqueness. Each person is truly beautiful not because of his or her physical attributes, but because he or she is made in God's image.

There's also another kind of beauty to consider—that of a person's character. When you think about dating someone or spending the rest of your life with that person, you'll have to look for more than physical beauty. If you want to build a relationship with someone, you'll have to communicate. If you get married, you'll have to blend your personality, goals, opinions, etc., with those of your spouse. But even a good personality doesn't mean you're made for each other. You'll need to consider your spiritual compatibility. And you'll have to make sure God wants you together.

The only cement that can bond two people together for life is a mutual commitment to God and to each other. As you're dating, remember that it takes more than beauty or a pleasant temperament to add up to someone whose love will last. The woman in Proverbs 31 had something more. That's what you should look for in others and work toward yourself. Let your attractiveness come from your character. Look beyond others' faces and bodies to what's on the inside. It may surprise you.

No Compromise

Bible Reading: Ephesians 5:1-18

Key Verse: *But do not let immorality or any impurity or greed even be named among you, as is proper among saints.*

Ephesians 5:3, NASB

Dating is important. Through dating you get to know

members of the opposite sex, and you may eventually find the person you want to marry. But dating is also tough—there's your self-concept to deal with, temptations, relationships that become problems, people you *don't* want to date, etc. So what should be your perspective?

First of all, don't let the amount of dating you do determine your self-concept or your view of your potential for marriage or a successful life.

Second, before you begin dating or before you go on any more dates, set some standards and put them in writing. Dating standards are choices you make about dating, based on the Bible, that you will put into practice. They are standards that you will not compromise, no matter what. Why? Because standards keep you from slipping. They help you stay out of high-pressure situations. They enable you to make good decisions now, not in the pressure of the moment. They help you consider what's truly important, and they help you stay close to Christ.

So what kinds of standards should you set? You'll need to decide what the Bible says about questions such as Should I date non-Christians? What about a physical relationship—how far is too far? What does God say about how I should live? Make a commitment to God right now that you won't let your physical relationship with another person get out of control. With the help of your parents or a youth leader, decide where to draw the line, and commit yourself to never cross it. Then consider the following personal concerns: how to say yes or no when asked on a date, or how to ask someone out; how to be creative in your dating so you'll have fun; who will pay and when; what things you want to do in your life before marriage (such as going to college); how involved you really want to get with one person as opposed to getting to know lots of people. Ask your parents for advice and opinions, and listen to them! Don't forget to ask for God's guidance, too.

If you take the time to think through your standards, then dating will be a fun chance to get to know people, in groups and in one-on-one situations. Chances are you'll find your future spouse through dating, so have fun, but take it seriously.

CHECK IT OUT:

Proverbs 7:6-21. *The glamour of sex leads to sin.*
Amos 3:3. *Christians should not date non-Christians.*
Romans 12:1-2. *God is in charge of your body.*
2 Corinthians 6:14-18. *Date other Christians.*
Philippians 4:13. *Let Christ guide your dating life.*
James 4:4. *Never compromise your beliefs on a date.*
1 Peter 3:3-4. *Be beautiful inside.*

DEATH

It's OK to Grieve

Bible Reading: 2 Samuel 1:1-16

Key Verse: *And they mourned and wept and fasted until evening for Saul and for Jonathan his son . . . because they had fallen by the sword.* 2 Samuel 1:12, NKJV

David and his men were visibly shaken over Saul's death: "They mourned and wept and fasted all day." This showed their genuine sorrow over the loss of their king, their friend Jonathan, and the other soldiers of Israel who died that day. They were not ashamed to grieve.

Today, expressing our emotions outwardly is considered by some to be a sign of weakness. Those who wish to appear strong try to hide their grief. But mourning can help us deal with our intense sorrow when a loved one dies.

Dealing with Suicide

Bible Reading: Jeremiah 20:14-18

Key Verse: *Why did I ever come out of the womb to see trouble and sorrow and to end my days in shame?* Jeremiah 20:18, NIV

Have you ever felt as Jeremiah did—wishing you'd never been born? Maybe you or someone you know has gone so far as to contemplate suicide. You may even know someone who has taken the next step. But what does God say about suicide? God is the author of life. To try to correct his "mistake" in making you by killing yourself is to play God—and he doesn't take that lightly. Suicide is a sin because it goes against God. But it isn't the unforgivable sin. While the person who commits suicide cannot ask for forgiveness, we must remember that we are not forgiven because of our faultless record of confession. Our past, present, and future sins are covered because of Christ's death for us.

Besides this, suicide doesn't solve any problems. In fact, it's one of the most selfish, cowardly, and hateful acts anyone can commit. And it causes overwhelming heartbreak and pain for those left behind.

So what do you do when you—or someone you care about—decide to simply end it all? First, remember you're not alone. Everyone has felt worthless at times. If others can make it, so can you. Second, don't lose hope. Things will get better—sometimes it just takes time. Third, know the danger signs that indicate someone might be considering suicide: going through a family crisis; being the victim of abuse or neglect; drug abuse; death of someone close; preoccupation with death and/or talk of suicide. If you or a friend are experiencing one or more of these signs, talk to someone you can trust—someone trained to help you. Last, remember that even if it seems that no one cares, Jesus does. Pour out your troubles to him. He understands because he, too, has experienced the depths of human despair. He is wonderfully able to help.

Afraid of Dying

Bible Reading: 1 Thessalonians 4:13–5:11

Key Verse: *But we do not want you to be uninformed, brothers and sisters, about those who have died, so that you may not grieve as others do who have no hope.*

1 Thessalonians 4:13, NRSV

Even Christians, who know they're going to heaven, may feel afraid when they think about dying—because death is an unknown. It leaves us with many unanswered questions: How will I die? What will be on the other side? Will the people I leave behind be OK? What if I die before I have the chance to experience all that I want to experience?

Death is not something that Christians have to fear, because for them death is not the end of the story. It is the gateway to a place of indescribable joy and beauty. It's the beginning of a new life. As you spend time in the Bible and with other Christians who have the same hope you do, you will grow to realize that death is only a door to an eternity far better than your wildest dreams!

CHECK IT OUT:

Ecclesiastes 9:10. *Death ends only earthly life.*

1 Corinthians 15:51-58. *Jesus has given us victory over death.*

2 Corinthians 5:15. *We will be with the Lord when we die.*

2 Timothy 1:10. *Jesus broke the power of death.*

Hebrews 9:27. *There is no reincarnation.*

1 John 4:17. *Don't fear death.*

Revelation 21:3-4. *There will be no more sorrow or tears in heaven.*

DECISIONS
Avoiding Conflict

Bible Reading: Numbers 20:14-29

Key Verse: *Please let us pass through your land. We shall not pass through field or through vineyard; we shall not even drink water from a well. We shall go along the king's highway, not turning to the right or left, until we pass through your territory.* Numbers 20:17, NASB

Moses negotiated and reasoned with the Edomite king. When nothing worked, he was left with two choices—force a conflict or avoid it. Moses knew there would be enough barriers in the days and months ahead. There was no point in adding another one unnecessarily. Sometimes conflict is unavoidable. At the same time, it may not be worth the consequences. Open warfare may seem heroic, courageous, and even righteous, but it is not always the best choice. The next time you encounter conflict, consider Moses' example and look for a peaceful solution to the problem.

Confessing Sin

Bible Reading: Deuteronomy 29:16-29

Key Verse: *Make sure there is no man or woman, clan or tribe among you today whose heart turns away from the LORD our God to go and worship the gods of those nations; make sure there is no root among you that produces such bitter poison.* Deuteronomy 29:18, NIV

Moses cautioned that the day the Hebrews chose to turn from God, a seed would be planted that would produce bitter fruit. When we decide to do what we know is wrong, we plant an evil seed that begins to grow out of control, eventually yielding a crop of sorrow and pain. But we can prevent those seeds of sin from taking root. If you have done something wrong, confess it to God and others immediately. If the seed never finds fertile soil, its bitter fruit will never ripen.

Get Good Advice

Bible Reading: 2 Chronicles 10:1-14

Key Verse: *The king answered them harshly. Rejecting the advice of the elders, he followed the advice of the young men.* 2 Chronicles 10:13-14, NIV

Following bad advice can cause disaster. Rehoboam lost the chance to rule a peaceful, united kingdom because he rejected the advice of Solomon's older counselors, preferring that of his peers. Rehoboam made two errors in seeking advice: (1) He did not give extra consideration to the suggestions of those who knew the situation better than he, and (2) he did not ask God for wisdom to discern which was the better option.

Like Rehoboam, we find it easy to follow the advice of our peers because they often feel as we do. But their view may be limited. It is important to listen carefully to those who have more experience than we do and can therefore see the bigger picture.

Make Good Choices, No Matter What the Cost

Bible Reading: 2 Chronicles 25:1-12

Key Verse: *Then Amaziah said to the man of God, "But what shall we do about the hundred talents which I have given to the troops of Israel?" And the man of God answered, "The LORD is able to give you much more than this."*

2 Chronicles 25:9, NKJV

Amaziah made a financial agreement with wicked Israelite soldiers, offering to pay them to fight for him (25:6). But before they went to battle, Amaziah sent them home with their pay after the prophet's warning. Although it cost him plenty, he wisely realized that the money was not worth the ruin the alliance could cause. How would you have chosen? Money must never stand in the way of making right decisions. The Lord's blessing is priceless, worth more than any amount of money.

Examine Your Motives

Bible Reading: Proverbs 21:1-8

Key Verse: *All deeds are right in the sight of the doer, but the LORD weighs the heart.* Proverbs 21:2, NRSV

People can find an excuse for doing almost anything, but God looks behind the excuse to the motives. We often have to make difficult choices in areas of life where the right action is difficult to discern. We can help ourselves make such decisions by trying to identify our motives first and then asking, "Would God be pleased with my real reasons for doing this?" God is not pleased when we do good deeds only to receive something back.

Follow Jesus' Example

Bible Reading: John 5:17-29

Key Verse: *I say to you, the Son can do nothing of Himself, unless it is something He sees the Father doing; for whatever the Father does, these things the Son also does in like manner.* John 5:19, NASB

Because of his unity with God, Jesus lived as God wanted him to live. Because of our identification with Jesus, we must live as he wants us to live. Asking ourselves the questions What would Jesus do? and What would Jesus have me do? may help us make the right choices.

How to Make Good Decisions

Bible Reading: Acts 1:14-26

Key Verses: *Therefore, of these men who have accompanied us all the time that the Lord Jesus went in and out among us, . . . one of these must become a witness with us.* Acts 1:21-22, NKJV

The apostles had to choose a replacement for Judas Iscariot. They outlined specific criteria for making the choice. When the "finalists" had been chosen, the apostles prayed, asking God to guide the selection process. This gives us a good example of how to proceed when we are making important decisions. Set up criteria consistent with biblical principles, examine the alternatives, and pray for wisdom and guidance to reach a wise decision.

CHECK IT OUT:

Deuteronomy 30:19-20. *Choose God's blessings.*
Joshua 24:15. *Choose to serve God.*
1 Samuel 15:1-35. *Choose to obey God daily.*
Esther 3–4. *Take a stand for what's right.*
Proverbs 8:1-21. *Choose wisdom over foolishness.*
Ecclesiastes 11:7–12:1. *Choose to honor God while you're young.*
Matthew 12:30. *Decide to be for Jesus or against him.*
Luke 6:12-16. *Jesus prayed before making decisions.*

Hebrews 11:13-16. *Decide to live God's way.*
James 1:5. *Use wisdom when making decisions.*
2 Peter 1:5-11. *Choose God's way.*

DEPRESSION

The Valley after the Mountaintop

Bible Reading: 1 Kings 19:1-18

Key Verse: *"I have had enough, LORD," he said. "Take my life; I am no better than my ancestors."*   1 Kings 19:4, NIV

Elijah experienced the depths of fatigue and discouragement just after his two great spiritual victories: the defeat of the prophets of Baal and the answered prayer for rain. Often discouragement sets in after great spiritual experiences, especially those requiring physical effort or producing emotional excitement. To lead him out of depression, God first let Elijah rest and eat. Then God confronted him with the need to return to his mission in life—to be God's prophet. Elijah's battles were not over. There was still work for him to do. When you feel let down after a great spiritual experience, remember that God's purpose for your life is not yet over.

Don't Give Up

Bible Reading: Job 6:8-30

Key Verses: *O that I might have my request, and that God would grant my desire; that it would please God to crush me, that he would let loose his hand and cut me off!*
    Job 6:8-9, NRSV

In his grief, Job wanted to give in, to be freed from his discomfort, and to die. But God did not grant Job's request. He had a greater plan for him. Our tendency, like Job's, is to want to give up and get out when the going gets rough. To trust God in the good times is commendable, but to trust him during the difficult times tests us to our limits and exercises our faith. In your struggles, whether large or small, trust that God is in control (Romans 8:28).

Meditate on God's Goodness

Bible Reading: Psalm 42:1-11

Key Verse: *O my God, my soul is cast down within me; therefore I will remember You from the land of the Jordan, and from the heights of Hermon, from the Hill Mizar.*

Psalm 42:6, NKJV

Depression is one of the most common emotional ailments. One cure for depression is to meditate on the record of God's goodness to his people. This will take your mind off the present situation and give you hope that it will improve. It focuses your thoughts on God's ability to help you rather than on your inability to help yourself. When you feel depressed, take advantage of this psalm's antidepressant. Read the Bible's accounts of God's goodness, and meditate on them.

When You're Down in the Dumps

Bible Reading: Psalm 88:1-18

Key Verse: *O LORD, the God who saves me, day and night I cry out before you.* Psalm 88:1, NIV

When people are down in the dumps or in the depths of despair, a common reaction is to feel like there's no reason to keep on going. They become immobilized. They struggle with the depression and may even struggle with guilt about being so depressed.

Christians are not immune to depression. We live in a broken world. Bad things happen to good people. We will get hurt and may respond in depression. Believers will face times of anxiety, despair, and darkness. Feeling down—really down—seems to be an occasional fact of life. Obviously depression that is too deep or lasts too long indicates a need for counseling. But there is nothing unusual or unspiritual about feeling low from time to time. If you struggle with depression, you're not alone. Like the psalmist, you can pour out your heart to God. Follow God. He listens and cares and will guide you safely through the dark valley.

CHECK IT OUT:

Proverbs 15:13. *Smile.*
Proverbs 17:22. *Find ways to be cheerful.*
Isaiah 1:18. *Trust in Christ to help beat depression.*
Lamentations 3:15-26. *God's compassion never ends.*
Ezekiel 36:25. *Be positive, enthusiastic, and happy.*
John 16:33. *Everyone gets depressed at times.*

(see also Discouragement, Failure, and Problems)

DEVOTIONS (SEE BIBLE)

DISCIPLINE

God Means What He Says

Bible Reading: Ezekiel 5:1-13

Key Verse: *Thus shall My anger be spent, and I will cause My fury to rest upon them, and I will be avenged; and they shall know that I, the LORD, have spoken it in My zeal, when I have spent My fury upon them.* Ezekiel 5:13, NKJV

Have you ever seen someone try to discipline a child by saying, "If you do that one more time . . ."? If the parent doesn't follow through, the child learns not to listen. Empty threats backfire. God was going to punish the Israelites for their blatant sins, and he wanted them to know that he would do what he said. The people learned the hard way that God always follows through on his word. Too many people ignore God's warnings that he will punish sin, treating them as empty threats. But God says, "What I threaten, I will do." Don't make the mistake of thinking that God doesn't really mean what he says.

A Sign of God's Love

Bible Reading: Amos 9:8-15

Key Verse: *"Surely the eyes of the Sovereign LORD are on the sinful kingdom. I will destroy it from the face of the earth—yet I will not totally destroy the house of Jacob," declares the LORD.*   Amos 9:8, NIV

Amos assured the Israelites that God's punishment would not be permanent. God wants to redeem, not punish. But when punishment is necessary, he doesn't withhold it. Like a loving father, God disciplines those he loves in order to correct them. If he disciplines you, accept it as a sign of his love.

CHECK IT OUT:

Deuteronomy 25:1-3. *Discipline should fit the offense.*
Proverbs 13:24. *Discipline shows love.*
Matthew 18:15-17. *Jesus has given us steps to follow for church discipline.*
Ephesians 6:4. *Do not discipline in anger.*
Hebrews 12:7-13. *Accept God's discipline.*
Revelation 3:19. *God disciplines his children.*

DISCOURAGEMENT

Act, Don't React

Bible Reading: Exodus 1:22–2:9

Key Verse: *When she could hide him no longer she got a papyrus basket for him, and plastered it with bitumen and pitch; she put the child in it and placed it among the reeds on the bank of the river.*   Exodus 2:3, NRSV

Moses' mother knew how wrong it would be to destroy her child. But there was little she could do to change Pharaoh's new law. Her only alternative was to hide the child and later place him in a tiny reed basket on the river. God used her courageous act to place her son, the Hebrew of his choice, in the house of Pharaoh. Do you sometimes feel surrounded by evil and frustrated by how little you can do about it? When faced with evil, look for ways to act against it. Then trust God to use your effort, however small it seems, in his war against evil.

When You Feel Overwhelmed

Bible Reading: Nehemiah 4:1-14

Key Verse: *Meanwhile, the people in Judah said, "The strength of the laborers is giving out, and there is so much rubble that we cannot rebuild the wall."*

Nehemiah 4:10, NIV

Accomplishing any large task is tiring. There are always pressures that bring discouragement—the task seems impossible, it can never be finished, or too many things are working against you. The only cure for fatigue and discouragement is focusing on God's purposes. Nehemiah reminded the workers of their calling, their goal, and God's protection. If you are overwhelmed by, tired of, or discouraged by an assignment, remember God's purpose for your life and the special purpose he has for the project.

When Life Just Seems Unfair

Bible Reading: Job 10:1-12

Key Verse: *My soul loathes my life; I will give free course to my complaint, I will speak in the bitterness of my soul.*

Job 10:1, NKJV

When we face baffling affliction, a natural response is to feel sorry for ourselves. Pain pushes us toward self-pity. At this point we are only one step from self-righteousness, where we keep track of life's injustices and say, "Look what happened to me; how unfair it is!" This comes close to saying God is unfair. Remember that life's trials, whether allowed by God or sent by God, can be the means for spiritual development and refinement. When facing difficult situations, ask yourself, "What can I learn, and how can I grow?" rather than "Who did this to me, and how can I get out of it?"

When the Problems Are Too Big

Bible Reading: Habakkuk 3:8-19

Key Verse: *The Sovereign LORD is my strength; he makes my feet like the feet of a deer, he enables me to go on the heights.*
Habakkuk 3:19, NIV

Crop failure and the death of flocks would devastate Judah. But Habakkuk affirmed that even in the midst of starvation, he would still rejoice in the Lord. Habakkuk's feelings were not controlled by the events around him, but by faith in God's ability to give him strength. When nothing seems to make sense, and when troubles seem to be more than you can handle, remember that God gives strength. Take your eyes off of your difficulties, and look to God. We cannot see all that God is doing, and we cannot see all that God will do. But we can be assured that he is God and will do what is right. Knowing this brings us confidence and hope in the midst of a confusing world.

When You Don't See Results

Bible Reading: 1 Corinthians 15:51-58

Key Verse: *Therefore, my beloved, be steadfast, immovable, always excelling in the work of the Lord, because you know that in the Lord your labor is not in vain.*
1 Corinthians 15:58, NRSV

Paul said that, because of the Resurrection, nothing we do is wasted. Sometimes we hesitate to do good because we don't see any results. But if we can maintain a heavenly perspective, we will understand that we don't often see the good that results from our efforts. Truly believing that Christ has won the ultimate victory will affect the way we live right now. Don't let discouragement over an apparent lack of results keep you from working. Do the good that you have opportunity to do, knowing that your work will have eternal results.

CHECK IT OUT:

Genesis 37:4. *Injustice can cause discouragement.*
Job 1:18-22. *Be faithful and not discouraged.*

Matthew 10:16-28. *Don't be discouraged by persecution.*
John 15:18. *Jesus knows about discouragement.*
Philippians 1:15-18. *Turn discouragement into victory.*

(see also Depression, Failure, and Problems)

DIVORCE

What Does God Say?

Bible Reading: Matthew 19:1-12

Key Verses: *"For this reason a man will leave his father and mother*
and be united to his wife, and the two will become one
flesh." . . . Therefore what God has joined together, let
man not separate.   Matthew 19:5-6, NIV

Chances are you know someone who's getting a
divorce. You may even know lots of people who are
divorced. Why is it that divorce is becoming so commonplace in our society? Is it possible to marry and
stay together for life? And what does God say about
divorce?

God created marriage (see Genesis 2:18), and for
this reason no one should enter it lightly—or exit it
lightly. People created divorce. Divorce was never in
God's plan. But because we are sinful, fallen people,
and our fallen nature affects every area of our lives,
including marriage, God has allowed for divorce
in some situations. Some marriage relationships
become so badly damaged (through sexual immorality,
desertion, abuse, or betrayal) that it's almost impossible
to heal them. At those times, God has allowed for
divorce. Even so, divorce is always painful, destructive,
and damaging.

If this makes you slightly hesitant about marriage—
good. That is a healthy hesitation to have. Not
because you should fear marriage, but because you
shouldn't rush into it. Never approach marriage with
the attitude, "Oh well, if it doesn't work out, there's
always divorce." When a man and woman get married
and say the words "till death do us part," they make a

covenant that they should not break. While divorce may be necessary in some cases, it is never God's first choice, and neither should it be ours.

CHECK IT OUT:

Malachi 2:13-17. *God hates divorce.*
Matthew 5:31-32. *Jesus spoke against divorce.*
1 Corinthians 7:1-17. *Paul gives advice about marriage.*

(see also Marriage)

DOUBTS

Turn to God with Your Doubts

Bible Reading: Matthew 11:1-15
Key Verse: *Are You the Coming One, or do we look for another?*
Matthew 11:3, NKJV

As John sat in prison, he began to experience some doubts about whether Jesus really was the Messiah. If John's purpose was to prepare people for the coming Messiah, and if Jesus really was that Messiah, then why was John in prison when he could have been preaching to the crowds, preparing their hearts?

Jesus answered John's doubts by pointing to his acts of healing the blind, lame, and deaf; curing the lepers; raising the dead; and preaching the Good News about God. With so much evidence, Jesus' identity was obvious. If you sometimes doubt your salvation, the forgiveness of your sins, or God's work in your life, look at the evidence in Scripture and the changes in your life. When you doubt, don't turn away from Christ; turn *to* him.

About Jesus' Resurrection

Bible Reading: Acts 1:1-11
Key Verse: *After his suffering, he showed himself to these men and gave many convincing proofs that he was alive. He appeared to them over a period of forty days and spoke about the kingdom of God.* Acts 1:3, NIV

Today there are still people who doubt Jesus' resurrection. But Jesus appeared to the apostles and more than five hundred believers (1 Corinthians 15:5-8) after his resurrection, proving that he was alive. Look at the change the Resurrection made in the disciples' lives. At Jesus' death, they scattered. They were disillusioned and feared for their lives. But after seeing the resurrected Christ, they were fearless and risked everything to spread the Good News about him around the world. They faced imprisonment, beatings, rejection, and martyrdom, yet they never compromised their mission. These men would not have risked their lives for something they knew was a fraud. They knew Jesus was raised from the dead, and the early church was fired with their enthusiasm to tell others. The Resurrection is a historical fact. Don't be discouraged by doubters who deny the Resurrection. Be filled with hope by the knowledge that one day you, and they, will stand before the living proof when Christ returns.

About Whether God Cares

Bible Reading: Acts 14:1-18

Key Verse: *Yet he has not left himself without a witness in doing good—giving you rains from heaven and fruitful seasons, and filling you with food and your hearts with joy.* Acts 14:17, NRSV

Responding to the people of Lystra, Paul and Barnabas reminded them that God never leaves himself "without a witness." Rain and crops, for example, demonstrate God's goodness. Later Paul wrote that this evidence in nature leaves people without an excuse for unbelief (Romans 1:20). When in doubt about God, look around and you will see plenty of evidence that he is at work in our world.

About Jesus' Life

Bible Reading: Acts 26:24-32

Key Verse: *Indeed the king knows about these things, and to him I speak freely; for I am certain that none of these things has escaped his notice, for this was not done in a corner.*

Acts 26:26, NRSV

Paul was appealing to the *facts*—people were still alive who had heard Jesus and seen his miracles. The empty tomb could still be seen, and the Christian message was turning the world upside down (17:6). The history of Jesus' life and the early church are facts that are still open for us to examine. We still have eyewitness accounts of Jesus' life in the Bible, as well as historical and archaeological records of the early church to study. Examine the events and facts as verified by many witnesses. Reconfirm your faith with the truth of these accounts.

CHECK IT OUT:

Genesis 17:15-21; 18:10-14. *Don't doubt; nothing is too hard for God.*

Joshua 1:9. *Banish doubt.*

Matthew 11:1-6. *How Jesus helped remove John's doubts.*

John 20:24-29. *We are blessed because we believe.*

James 1:5-8. *Don't let doubt ruin your faith.*

Jude 1:22. *Be merciful toward those who doubt.*

(see also Faith and Trust)

DRINKING

Getting Lost in Alcohol

Bible Reading: Proverbs 23:29-35

Key Verse: *Do not gaze at wine when it is red, when it sparkles in the cup, when it goes down smoothly!*   Proverbs 23:31, NIV

Besides the certain hangovers and the true horror of deaths due to drunken driving, alcohol is simply addicting. After a while you need more and more to get the desired "buzz." Then it becomes a way to drown out life's everyday problems. But the soothing comfort of alcohol is only temporary. Real relief comes from dealing with the cause of the problem and turning to God for peace. Don't lose yourself in alcohol—find your life and peace in God.

CHECK IT OUT:

Genesis 9:20-27. *Drinking alcohol causes trouble.*

Esther 1:10–2:1. *Drinking can cause bad decisions.*

Proverbs 2:1-15. *Use God's wisdom to battle evil.*

Proverbs 20:1. *Only foolish people get drunk.*

Proverbs 31:4-7. *Drinking has many dangers.*

Isaiah 5:22. *Woe to those who drink.*

Luke 21:34. *Don't carouse and drink.*

Romans 13:11-14. *Don't get drunk.*

1 Corinthians 10:31. *Glorify God in all you do.*

1 Corinthians 10:32. *Your actions could make others stumble.*

Ephesians 5:18. *Many evils lie along the path of drinking.*

(see also Drugs, Partying, and Peer Pressure)

DRUGS

What's Wrong with Drugs

Bible Reading: 1 Corinthians 6:19-20; Galatians 5:19-20

Key Verse: *Or do you not know that your body is a temple of the Holy Spirit who is in you, whom you have from God, and that you are not your own?* 1 Corinthians 6:19, NASB

What's so bad about using drugs? Part of the answer involves the fact that drugs (whether crack, marijuana, steroids, or even paint fumes) damage the human body. If you're a Christian, your body doesn't belong to you. God owns it, and he tells you to take care of it.

Another reason not to do drugs is found in Galatians 5:19. Here Paul warns people against the sin of *spiritism* (encouraging the activity of demons). The Greek word for *spiritism* actually comes from the Greek noun *pharmakeia,* from which we get the word *pharmacy* (better known as a drug store). When most of the Bible was translated, drug problems were not common, but there was "spiritism."

The connection is inescapable. Spiritism (sorcery, witchcraft) actually happens when drugs that alter people's emotions, reflexes, and brain waves are taken. Taking drugs is like opening your subconscious to demons! That's why it's so dangerous.

Although many may laugh at this explanation, it's a message that must be given to those who are taking drugs. Keep your mind sharp and alert. Don't ruin it (and your life) with drugs.

CHECK IT OUT:

1 Corinthians 10:31. *Glorify God in all you do.*
1 Corinthians 10:32. *Your actions could make others stumble.*

(see also Drinking and Partying)

EDUCATION

Open to Instruction

Bible Reading: Daniel 12:1-13

Key Verse: *None of the wicked will understand, but those who are wise will understand.* Daniel 12:10, NIV

Daniel was told that to understand what is happening, people have to be open to instruction. Trials and persecutions, when we are in the middle of them, make very little sense. But they can purify us if we are willing to learn from them. After you survive a difficult time, seek to learn from it so that it can help you in the future.

Eager to Learn?

Bible Reading: Acts 10:28-48

Key Verse: *And he ordered them to be baptized in the name of Jesus Christ. Then they asked him to stay on for a few days.* Acts 10:48, NASB

Cornelius wanted Peter to stay with him for several days. As a new believer, Cornelius realized his need for teaching and fellowship. Are you that eager to learn more about Christ? Recognize your need to fellowship with and learn from more mature Christians. Then make the time to be with them.

Compare Teaching with God's Word

Bible Reading: Acts 17:1-12

Key Verse: *These Jews were more receptive than those in Thessalonica, for they welcomed the message very eagerly and examined the scriptures every day to see whether these things were so.* Acts 17:11, NRSV

How do you evaluate sermons and teachings? The people in Beroea opened the Scriptures for themselves and searched for truths to verify or disprove the message they heard. Always compare what you hear with what the Bible says. A preacher or teacher who gives God's true message will never contradict or explain away anything in God's Word.

Don't Turn Off Your Mind

Bible Reading: Acts 18:22-28

Key Verse: *For he vigorously refuted the Jews publicly, showing from the Scriptures that Jesus is the Christ.* Acts 18:28, NKJV

Apollos was from Alexandria in Egypt, the second largest city in the Roman Empire and home of a great university. He was a scholar, orator, and debater. After his knowledge about Christ was made more complete, God greatly used Apollos's gifts to strengthen and encourage the church. Reason is a powerful tool in the right hands and the right situation. Apollos used his reasoning ability to convince many in Greece of the truth of the gospel. You don't have to turn off your mind when you turn to Christ. If you have an ability in logic or debate, use it to bring others to God.

CHECK IT OUT:

Deuteronomy 11:16-21. *Education should be continual.*
Psalm 78:1-8. *Christian education should start at home.*
Proverbs 13:14. *Make education refreshing and encouraging.*
Lamentations 3:27-33. *Useful learning involves truth.*
Matthew 5-7. *Jesus taught with truth.*

ETERNAL LIFE

On God's Mercy Alone

Bible Reading: Deuteronomy 9:1-7

Key Verse: *Know, then, it is not because of your righteousness that the LORD your God is giving you this good land to possess, for you are a stubborn people.* Deuteronomy 9:6, NASB

If the Israelites were so wicked and stubborn, why did God make such wonderful promises to them? There are two good reasons: (1) A bargain is a bargain. God and Israel had made a covenant (Genesis 15; 17; Exodus 19–20). God promised to be faithful to them, and they promised to obey him. The agreement was irrevocable and eternal. Even though the Israelites rarely upheld their end of the bargain, God would always be faithful to his part. (Although he has punished them several times, he always has remained faithful.) (2) God's mercy is unconditional. No matter how many times the people turned from God, he was always there to restore them. It is comforting to know that, despite our inconsistencies and sins, God loves us unconditionally. Eternal life is not achieved on the merit system, but on the mercy system. God loves us no matter who we are or what we have done.

A Certain Hope

Bible Reading: Job 14:1-14

Key Verse: *If a man dies, shall he live again? All the days of my hard service I will wait, till my change comes.* Job 14:14, NKJV

Job lamented that life is brief and full of trouble. Sickness, loneliness, disappointment, and death caused him to say that life is not fair. Still, he clung to the one truth that also gives hope to us—resurrection. God's solution to an unfair world is to guarantee life with him forever. No matter how unfair your present world seems, God offers the hope of being in his presence eternally.

No One Can Take It Away

Bible Reading: John 9:1-34

Key Verse: *His parents said this because they were afraid of the Jews; for the Jews had already agreed that anyone who confessed Jesus to be the Messiah would be put out of the synagogue.* John 9:22, NRSV

The man's new faith was severely tested by some of the

authorities. He was cursed and evicted from the synagogue. You also may expect persecution when you follow Jesus. You may lose friends. You may even lose your life. But no one can ever take away the eternal life you have been given by Jesus.

You Know It

Bible Reading: 1 John 5:1-15

Key Verse: *I write these things to you who believe in the name of the Son of God, so that you may know that you have eternal life.*   1 John 5:13, NRSV

Some people *hope* they will be given eternal life. John says that we can *know* we have it. Our certainty is based on God's promise that he has given us eternal life through his Son. This is true whether you feel close to God or distant from him. Eternal life is not based on feelings, but on facts. You can know you have eternal life if you believe God's truth. If you lack assurance as to whether you are a Christian, ask yourself if you have honestly committed your life to Christ as your Savior and Lord. If so, you know by faith that you are indeed a child of God.

More Wonderful

Bible Reading: Revelation 21:1-27

Key Verse: *And God will wipe away every tear from their eyes; there shall be no more death, nor sorrow, nor crying. There shall be no more pain, for the former things have passed away.*   Revelation 21:4, NKJV

Have you ever wondered what eternity will be like? The "Holy City, the new Jerusalem," is described as the place where God "will wipe away all tears." Forevermore, there will be no death, pain, sorrow, or crying. What a wonderful truth! No matter what you are going through, it's not the last word. God has written the final chapter, and it includes eternal joy for those who love him. We do not know as much as we would like, but it is enough to know that eternity with God will be more wonderful than we can imagine.

CHECK IT OUT:

Psalm 39:1-6. *Thinking about eternal life lessens troubles.*
Proverbs 11:30. *Tell others about eternal life.*
Matthew 7:13-14. *Jesus is the only way to eternal life.*
John 5:24; 6:68. *Those who believe in Jesus have eternal life.*
Romans 6:23. *Eternal life is God's gift.*
Ephesians 2:8-9. *You can't earn eternal life.*
1 John 2:24-25. *God has promised us eternal life.*
Revelation 3:5. *Those who overcome will have eternal life.*

EXCUSES

You Should Know Better

Bible Reading: Judges 16:4-21

Key Verse: *With such nagging she prodded him day after day until he was tired to death.* Judges 16:16, NIV

Delilah kept asking Samson for the secret of his strength until he finally grew tired of hearing her nagging and gave in. What a pitiful excuse for disobedience! Don't allow anyone, no matter how attractive or persuasive, to talk you into doing wrong.

You Can't Hide from God

Bible Reading: 1 Samuel 13:1-14

Key Verse: *I thought, "Now the Philistines will come down against me at Gilgal, and I have not sought the LORD's favor." So I felt compelled to offer the burnt offering.*
1 Samuel 13:12, NIV

Saul had plenty of excuses for his disobedience. But Samuel zeroed in on the real issue: "You have disobeyed the commandment of the Lord your God." Like Saul, we often gloss over our mistakes and sins, trying to justify and spiritualize our actions because of our "special" circumstances. Our excuses, however, are nothing more than disobedience. God knows our true motives. He forgives, restores, and blesses only when we are honest about our sins. By trying to hide his sins behind excuses, Saul lost his kingship (13:14).

Irrational Rationalizations

Bible Reading: Ezekiel 9:1-10

Key Verse: *As for me, my eye will not spare, nor will I have pity, but I will bring down their deeds upon their heads.*
Ezekiel 9:10, NRSV

The people said that God had gone away and wouldn't see their sin. People have many convenient explanations to make it easier to sin: "It doesn't matter," "Everybody's doing it," or "Nobody will ever know." Do you find yourself making excuses for sin? Rationalizing makes it easier to commit sin. But rationalizing sin does not influence God to not punish it.

Not As Bad As Some People

Bible Reading: Mark 14:48-72

Key Verse: *"You have heard the blasphemy! What do you think?"*
And they all condemned Him to be deserving of death.
Mark 14:64, NKJV

It is easy to get angry at the Jewish Supreme Court for their injustice in condemning Jesus, but Peter and the rest of the disciples also contributed to Jesus' pain by deserting him. While most of us are not like the Jewish leaders, we are all like the disciples, for all of us have been guilty of denying Christ as Lord in vital areas of our lives. We may pride ourselves that we have not committed certain sins, but we are all guilty of sin. Don't excuse yourself by pointing the finger at others whose sins seem worse than yours.

CHECK IT OUT:

Genesis 3:12-13. *We tend to blame others for our sin.*
1 Kings 11:1-11. *Excused sin will ruin us in the end.*
Matthew 5:32. *Don't look for excuses to end your marriage.*

John 4:35. *Don't make excuses for not witnessing.*

Romans 1:18-20. *There is no excuse for not believing in God.*

Ephesians 5:5-9. *Don't be taken in by excuses.*

James 1:13-14. *There is no excuse when we sin.*

FAILURE

Learn from It

Bible Reading: Jeremiah 44:1-10

Key Verse: *Have you forgotten the crimes of your ancestors, . . .
which they committed in the land of Judah and in the
streets of Jerusalem?*   Jeremiah 44:9, NRSV

When we forget a lesson or refuse to learn it, we risk
repeating our mistakes. The people of Judah struggled
with this same matter—to forget their former sins was
to repeat them. To fail to learn from failure
is to assure future failure. Your past is your school
of experience. Let your past mistakes point you to
God's way.

Overcome It

Bible Reading: Luke 22:39-62

Key Verse: *So Peter went out and wept bitterly.*   Luke 22:62, NKJV

Peter wept bitterly, not only because he realized he
had denied his Lord, the Messiah, but also because he
had turned away from a very dear friend, a person
who had loved and taught him for three years. Peter
had said he would *never* deny Christ, despite Jesus'
prediction (22:34-35). But when Peter was frightened,
he went against all he had boldly promised. Unable
to stand up for his Lord for even twelve hours, Peter
had failed as a disciple and as a friend. From this
humiliating experience Peter learned much that
would help him in the leadership responsibilities he
would soon assume. We need to be aware of our own
breaking points and not become overconfident or
self-sufficient. If we fail, we must remember that
Christ can use those who recognize their failure for
his work and glory.

CHECK IT OUT:

> Numbers 14:17-18. *Parents' failures can affect children.*
> Joshua 7:25–8:1. *Turning failures into success.*
> Isaiah 42:18-25. *Learn from failures.*
> Matthew 1:1-17. *God can work through failure.*
>
> *(see also Depression, Discouragement, and Problems)*

FAIRNESS

Life Isn't Fair

Bible Reading: 1 Samuel 22:1-23

Key Verse: *But Abiathar, a son of Ahimelech son of Ahitub, escaped and fled to join David.* 1 Samuel 22:20, NIV

Why did God allow eighty-five innocent priests to be killed? Scripture does not give a specific answer to this question, but it gives insights into the issue. Serving God is not a ticket to wealth, success, or health. While God does not promise to protect good people from evil in this world, we can find comfort in knowing that he does promise that ultimately all evil will be abolished. Those who have remained faithful throughout their trials will experience untold blessings in the age to come (Matthew 5:11-12; Revelation 21:1-7; 22:1-21).

Do You Give It?

Bible Reading: Isaiah 11:1-9

Key Verse: *His delight shall be in the fear of the LORD. He shall not judge by what his eyes see, or decide by what his ears hear.* Isaiah 11:3, NRSV

How we long for fair treatment from others, but do we give it ourselves? We hate those who base their judgments on appearance, false evidence, or hearsay. But we can be quick to judge others using those same criteria. Only Christ can be the perfectly fair judge, and only as he governs our hearts can we learn to be as fair in our treatment of others as we expect others to be toward us.

Keep Your Promises

Bible Reading: Isaiah 33:1-9

Key Verse: *Woe to you, O destroyer, you who have not been destroyed! Woe to you, O traitor, you who have not been betrayed! When you stop destroying, you will be destroyed; when you stop betraying, you will be betrayed.*
Isaiah 33:1, NIV

The Assyrians continually broke their promises but demanded that others keep theirs. It is easy to put ourselves in the same selfish position, demanding our rights while violating the rights of others. Broken promises shatter trust and destroy relationships. Determine to not make promises that you can't keep. In addition, ask forgiveness for past promises you have broken. Exercise the same fairness with others that you demand for yourself.

God's Standards

Bible Reading: Ezekiel 18:23-32

Key Verse: *Yet you say, "The way of the Lord is not fair." Hear now, O house of Israel, is it not My way which is fair, and your ways which are not fair?*
Ezekiel 18:25, NKJV

A typical childish response to punishment is to say, "That isn't fair!" In reality, God is fair, but *we* have broken the rules. It is not God who must live up to our ideas of fairness. Instead, we must live up to his. Don't spend your time looking for the loopholes in God's law; decide instead to work toward living up to his standards.

CHECK IT OUT:

Psalm 58:1-11. *God hates unfairness.*
Psalm 73:1-28. *Sometimes wicked people prosper.*
Proverbs 16:11. *Be fair in business.*
Ecclesiastes 9:11. *Life isn't always fair.*
Isaiah 3:1-26. *God will punish injustice.*

Zechariah 7:8-14. *Don't take advantage of others.*
Matthew 5:38-48. *Jesus had a different approach to injustice.*

FAITH

We Can Do What God Commands

Bible Reading: 1 Kings 18:21-39

Key Verse: *And Elijah came near to all the people and said, "How long will you hesitate between two opinions? If the LORD is God, follow Him; but if Baal, follow him."*

1 Kings 18:21, NASB

Just as God caused fire to rain from heaven for Elijah, he will help us accomplish what he commands us to do. The proof may not be as dramatic in our lives as in Elijah's, but God will make resources available to us in creative ways to accomplish his purposes. He will give us the wisdom to raise a family, the courage to take a stand for truth, or the means to provide help for someone in need. Like Elijah, we can have faith that, whatever God commands us to do, he will provide what we need to carry it through.

Will You Believe and Obey?

Bible Reading: 2 Kings 4:1-7

Key Verse: *When all the jars were full, she said to her son, "Bring me another one." But he replied, "There is not a jar left." Then the oil stopped flowing.*   2 Kings 4:6, NIV

The woman and her sons collected pots and pans from their neighbors, and they began to pour oil into them from their one small jar. The oil stopped pouring only when they ran out of containers. The number of jars they gathered was an indication of their faith. God's provision was as large as their faith and willingness to obey. Beware of limiting God's blessings by a lack of faith and obedience.

What Faith Can Do

Bible Reading: 2 Kings 18:1-8; 20:1-7

Key Verse: *I will add fifteen years to your life. I will deliver you and this city out of the hand of the king of Assyria; I will defend this city for my own sake and for my servant David's sake.* 2 Kings 20:6, NRSV

Over a one-hundred-year period of Judah's history (732–640 B.C.), Hezekiah was the only faithful king. But what a difference he made! Because of Hezekiah's faith and prayer, God healed him and saved his city from the Assyrians. You can make a difference too, even if your faith puts you in the minority. Faith and prayer, if they are sincere and directed toward the one true God, can bring about change in any situation.

Set Apart by God

Bible Reading: Isaiah 10:20-23

Key Verse: *A remnant will return, a remnant of Jacob will return to the Mighty God.* Isaiah 10:21, NIV

Those who remained faithful to God despite the horrors of the invasion were called the remnant. The key to being a part of the remnant was *faith*. Being a descendant of Abraham, living in the Promised Land, having trusted God at one time—none of these were good enough. Are you relying on your Christian heritage, the rituals of worship, or past experiences to put you in a right relationship with God? The key to being set apart by God is faith in him.

Focus of Faith

Bible Reading: Matthew 14:23-33

Key Verse: *And Peter answered Him and said, "Lord, if it is You, command me to come to You on the water."* Matthew 14:28, NKJV

Peter was not testing Jesus, something we are told not to do (4:7). Instead, he was the only one in the boat to react in faith. His impulsive request led him to experience a rather unusual demonstration of God's power. But when Peter realized what he was doing, his faith wavered. Then Peter took his eyes off Jesus, focused on the high waves around him, and started to sink.

We may not walk on water, but we do walk through tough situations. If we focus on the waves of difficult circumstances around us without looking to Christ for help, we too may despair and sink. To maintain your faith in the midst of difficult situations, keep your eyes on Christ and his power rather than on your inadequacies.

Enough Faith?

Bible Reading: Romans 4:1-5

Key Verse: *But to the one who does not work, but believes in Him who justifies the ungodly, his faith is reckoned as righteousness.* Romans 4:5, NASB

Some people start to worry when they learn that they are saved through faith. *Do I have enough faith?* they wonder. *Is my faith strong enough to save me?* These people miss the point. It is Jesus Christ who saves us, not *our* feelings or actions, and he is strong enough to save us no matter how weak our faith is. Jesus offers us salvation as a gift because he loves us, not because we have earned it through our powerful faith. What, then, is the role of faith? Faith is believing and trusting in Jesus Christ, reaching out to accept his wonderful gift of salvation. Faith is effective whether it is great or small, timid or bold—because God loves us.

Never Disappointed

Bible Reading: Romans 9:30-33

Key Verse: *Why not? Because they pursued it not by faith but as if it were by works. They stumbled over the "stumbling stone."* Romans 9:32, NIV

Sometimes we are like these people, trying hard to get right with God by keeping his laws. We may think going to church, giving offerings, and being nice will be enough. After all, we've played by the rules, haven't we? But Paul says this approach never succeeds. He explains that God's plan of salvation is not for those who try to earn his favor by being good. Rather, it is for those who realize they can never be good enough and so must depend on Christ. Only by putting our faith in what Jesus Christ has done for us will we be saved. If we do that, we will never be disappointed.

Strong and Weak

Bible Reading: Romans 14:1-23

Key Verse: *For the kingdom of God is not eating and drinking, but righteousness and peace and joy in the Holy Spirit.*
                                                    Romans 14:17, NASB

Who is weak in faith, and who is strong? We are all weak in some areas and strong in others. Our faith is strong in an area if we can survive contact with temptation without falling into sin. It is weak if we must avoid certain activities or places in order to protect our spiritual life. It is important to take a self-inventory in order to find out where we are weak and where we are strong.

In areas of strength, we should not fear that we will be defiled by the world. Rather, from our position of strength we should lead the world. In areas of weakness, however, we need to play it safe. If we have a strong faith but shelter it, we are not doing Christ's work in the world. If we have a weak faith but expose it, we are being extremely foolish. Strengths and weaknesses are not permanent conditions. Strengths, however, may diminish if they are not put to the test, and weaknesses may develop by God's power into strengths.

Keep the Faith

Bible Reading: Hebrews 11:1-16

Key Verse: *Now faith is the assurance of things hoped for, the conviction of things not seen.*   Hebrews 11:1, NRSV

The people of faith listed in this chapter died without

receiving all that God had promised, but they never lost their vision of heaven. Many Christians become frustrated and defeated because their needs, wants, expectations, and demands were not immediately met when they believed in Christ. They become impatient and want to quit. Are you discouraged because your goal seems far away? Take courage from these heroes of faith who lived and died without seeing the fruit of their faith on earth yet continued to believe.

CHECK IT OUT:

Genesis 15:6. *Abraham is an example of faith.*

Matthew 8:5-13; John 20:24-31. *Real faith believes without seeing.*

Matthew 9:18-26. *Faith results in actions.*

Luke 17:6. *Even small faith is valuable.*

Romans 4:3-5. *Faith in God cleanses us from sin.*

Galatians 3:11. *We are saved by faith, not law keeping.*

(see also Belief and Trust)

FAMILY

Top Priority

Bible Reading: 1 Kings 5:1-18

Key Verses: *Then King Solomon raised up a labor force out of all Israel; and the labor force was thirty thousand men. And he sent them to Lebanon . . . in shifts: they were one month in Lebanon and two months at home.*

1 Kings 5:13-14, NKJV

Solomon drafted three times the number of workers needed for the temple project and then arranged their schedules so they didn't have to be away from home for long periods of time. This showed his concern for the welfare of his workers and the importance he placed on family life. The strength of a nation is in direct proportion to the strength of its families. Solomon wisely recognized that family should always be a top priority. As you structure your own work or arrange the schedules of others, be careful to limit the negative impact your plans have on your family as well as others' families.

What's Your Heritage?

Bible Reading: Ezekiel 18:14-22

Key Verse: *The soul who sins is the one who will die. The son will not share the guilt of the father, nor will the father share the guilt of the son. The righteousness of the righteous man will be credited to him, and the wickedness of the wicked will be charged against him.* Ezekiel 18:20, NIV

Family traditions were very important to the Jews, but God made it clear that people should not follow a tradition of sin. Although your family is a powerful influence in your life, your actions are not determined by them. You can choose not to follow a pattern of sin. Even if you come from a sinful family, you can follow God. It is far better to begin a new spiritual heritage than to hold on to traditions of sin.

Honor Your Family

Bible Reading: Luke 2:41-52

Key Verse: *Then he went down with them and came to Nazareth, and was obedient to them.* Luke 2:51, NRSV

This is the first hint that Jesus realized he was God's Son. But even though Jesus knew his real Father, he did not reject his earthly parents. Jesus went back to Nazareth with them and lived under their authority for another eighteen years. God's people do not despise human relationships or family responsibilities. If the Son of God obeyed his human parents, how much more should we honor our family members!

Potential Conflict

Bible Reading: Luke 12:35-53

Key Verse: *They will be divided, father against son, and son against father; mother against daughter, and daughter against mother.* Luke 12:53, NASB

In these unsettling words, Jesus revealed that his coming would often result in conflict. Because he demands a response, close groups can be torn apart when some choose to follow him and others refuse to do so. There is no middle ground with Jesus. Loyalties must be declared and commitments made, sometimes to the severing of other relationships. Life is easiest when a family unitedly believes in Christ, but this often does not happen. Are you willing to risk your family's approval to gain eternal life?

Love Your Family

Bible Reading: John 19:16-27

Key Verse: *Then He said to the disciple, "Behold your mother!" And from that hour that disciple took her to his own home.*

John 19:27, NKJV

Even while dying on the cross, Jesus was concerned about his family. He instructed John to care for Mary, Jesus' mother. Our families are precious gifts from God, and we should value and care for them under all circumstances. What can you do today to show your love to your family?

CHECK IT OUT:

Proverbs 5:15-21. *Spouses should love each other.*
Proverbs 11:29. *Never provoke your family to anger.*
Matthew 10:34-39. *Love and honor your family.*
Matthew 12:46-50. *Christians are adopted into God's family.*
Ephesians 2:19. *We are members of God's family.*
1 Timothy 5:3-5. *Never ignore your family.*
2 Timothy 1:5-8. *Share Christ with your family.*

FEAR

Facing a Difficult Conflict

Bible Reading: Genesis 32:3-12; 33:1-4

Key Verse: *Save me, I pray, from the hand of my brother Esau, for I am afraid he will come and attack me, and also the mothers with their children.* Genesis 32:11, NIV

How would you feel knowing you were about to meet the person you had cheated out of his or her most precious possession? Jacob had taken Esau's birthright (25:33) and his blessings (27:27-40). Now he was about to meet this brother for the first time in twenty years, and he was frantic with fear. He collected his thoughts, however, and decided to pray. When we face a difficult conflict, we can run about frantically, or we can pause to pray. Which approach will be more effective?

Facing a New Situation

Bible Reading: Genesis 46:1-7

Key Verse: *So He said, "I am God, the God of your father; do not fear to go down to Egypt, for I will make of you a great nation there."* Genesis 46:3, NKJV

God told Jacob to leave his home and travel to a strange and faraway land. But God reassured Jacob by promising to go with him and take care of him. When new situations or surroundings frighten or worry you, recognize that experiencing fear is normal. To be paralyzed by fear, however, is an indication that you question God's ability to take care of you.

Facing a Tough Challenge

Bible Reading: Numbers 13:17-33

Key Verse: *And they spread among the Israelites a bad report about the land they had explored.* Numbers 13:32, NIV

God told the Israelites that the Promised Land was rich and plentiful. Not only that, he promised that this bountiful land would be theirs. When the spies reported back to Moses, they gave plenty of good reasons for entering the land, but they couldn't stop focusing on their fear. Talk of giants and walled cities made it easy to forget about God's promise to help.

When facing tough decisions, weigh the positives and the negatives carefully. But don't let potential difficulties blind you to God's power to help and his promise to guide.

God Is Greater than Your Fears

Bible Reading: Nehemiah 2:1-6

Key Verse: *May the king live forever! Why should my face not be sad, when the city, the place of my fathers' tombs, lies waste, and its gates are burned with fire?* Nehemiah 2:3, NKJV

Nehemiah wasn't ashamed to admit his fear, but he refused to allow fear to stop him from doing what God had called him to do. When we allow our fears to rule our lives, we make them more powerful than God. Is there something God wants you to do, but fear is holding you back? God is greater than all our fears. Recognizing your fear is the first step in committing it to God. If God has called you to a task, he will help you to accomplish it.

Fear about the End of the World

Bible Reading: Psalm 46:1-11

Key Verse: *God is our refuge and strength, an ever-present help in trouble.* Psalm 46:1, NIV

The fear of mountains or cities suddenly crumbling into the sea by a nuclear blast haunts many people today. But the psalmist says that even if the world ends, "we need not fear!" Even in the face of utter destruction, he expressed a quiet confidence in God's ability to save him. It seems impossible to face the end of the world without fear, but the Bible is clear—God is our refuge even in the face of total destruction. He is not merely a temporary retreat. He is our eternal refuge and can provide strength even in the face of global destruction.

Fear of the Future

Bible Reading: Psalm 112:1-10

Key Verse: *He will not fear evil tidings; his heart is steadfast, trusting in the LORD.* Psalm 112:7, NASB

We all want to live without fear. In fact, we admire our heroes because we think they are fearless people who take on all dangers and overcome them. The psalmist teaches us that *fear* of God can lead to a *fearless* life. To fear God means to respect and reverence him as the almighty Lord. When we do this, we will begin to trust God completely to take care of us. Then we will find that our other fears—even of death itself—will subside.

Better to Obey than to Fear

Bible Reading: Jonah 1:1-17

Key Verse: *But Jonah rose up to flee to Tarshish from the presence of the Lord.* Jonah 1:3, NASB

Jonah was afraid. He knew that God had a specific job for him, but he didn't want to do it. Fear made him run. When God gives us directions through his Word, sometimes we run in fear, claiming that God is asking too much. But running got Jonah into worse trouble. In the end, he knew that it was best to do what God had asked in the first place. But by then he had paid a costly price for running. But, as Jonah learned, it is far better to obey God from the start.

CHECK IT OUT:

Genesis 15:1. *God gave Abram two reasons not to fear.*
Deuteronomy 1:19-26. *Trust God and his guidance.*
Joshua 1:9. *The Lord is with you.*
Psalm 25:12-14. *Fearing God means reverence and respect.*
Proverbs 29:25. *Don't fear people; trust God.*
Matthew 10:28. *Don't fear people; fear God alone.*
Luke 21:25-28. *Jesus is coming, so have no fear.*
Acts 5:17-29. *Faith overcomes fear.*

(see also Worry)

FORGIVENESS

God Gets the Stains Out

Bible Reading: Isaiah 1:16-31; 43:25

Key Verse: *"Come now, and let us reason together," says the Lord, "Though your sins are like scarlet, they shall be as white*

*as snow; though they are red like crimson, they shall be
as wool."* Isaiah 1:18, NKJV

A deep stain is virtually impossible to remove from
clothing, and the stain of sin seems equally permanent.
But God can remove the stain of sin from our lives just
as he promised to do for the Israelites. We don't have to
go through life permanently soiled. Through prayer we
can be assured that Christ has forgiven our worst sins
and removed our most indelible stains.

God Can Forgive All Your Sins

Bible Reading: Lamentations 3:21-26
Key Verses: *But this I call to mind, and therefore I have hope: The
steadfast love of the LORD never ceases, his mercies never
come to an end.* Lamentations 3:21-22, NRSV

Jeremiah saw one ray of hope in the midst of all the sin
and sorrow surrounding him: *God's compassion never
ends.* Compassion is love in action. God willingly
responds with help when we ask sincerely. Perhaps
there is some sin in your life that you thought God
would not forgive. God's compassion is greater than
any sin, and he promises forgiveness. Do you feel as
though God could never forgive you, that your sins are
too many, or that some of them are too great? The good
news is that God can and will forgive them all. Nobody
is beyond redemption, and nobody is so full of sin that
he or she cannot be made clean.

God Wants to Forgive You

Bible Reading: Ezekiel 33:1-20
Key Verse: *Say to them, "As I live!" declares the Lord GOD, "I take no
pleasure in the death of the wicked. . . . Turn back, turn
back from your evil ways!"* Ezekiel 33:11, NASB

The exiles were discouraged by their past sins. They felt
heavy guilt for living in rebellion against God for so
many years. This was an important turning point—else-
where in Ezekiel the people had refused to face their
sins. But God assured them of forgiveness if they

repented. God *wants* everyone to turn to him. He looks at what we are and will become, not what we have been. God gives every person the opportunity to turn to him, so take it. Sincerely try to follow him, and ask him to forgive you when you fail.

Only God Can Forgive

Bible Reading: Hosea 14:1-9

Key Verse: *Take words with you and return to the LORD; say to him, "Take away all guilt; accept that which is good, and we will offer the fruit of our lips."* Hosea 14:2, NRSV

The people could return to God by asking him to take away their sins. The same is true for us: We can pray Hosea's prayer and know our sins are forgiven because Christ paid the penalty for them on the cross (John 3:16).

When we request forgiveness, we must recognize that we do not deserve it and therefore cannot demand it. Our appeal must be for God's love and mercy, not for his justice. Although we cannot demand forgiveness, we can be confident we have received it, because God is gracious and loving and wants to restore us to himself, just as he wanted to restore Israel.

How We Should Forgive Others

Bible Reading: Matthew 18:15-35

Key Verse: *Jesus answered, "I tell you, not seven times, but seventy-seven times."* Matthew 18:22, NIV

The rabbis taught that Jews should forgive those who offended them three times. Peter, in trying to be especially generous, asked Jesus if seven (the "perfect" number) was enough times to forgive someone. But Jesus answered, "seventy-seven times," meaning that we shouldn't even keep track of how many times we forgive someone. We should always forgive those who are truly repentant, no matter how many times they ask.

Forgiving Others Brings Joy

Bible Reading: Luke 15:11-32

Key Verse: *But when this son of yours who has squandered your property with prostitutes comes home, you kill the fattened calf for him!* Luke 15:30, NIV

In the story of the Prodigal Son, there is a contrast between the father's response and the older brother's reaction. The father was forgiving and overjoyed. The brother was unforgiving and bitter. The father forgave because he was joyful, and the son refused to forgive because he was bitter. The difference between bitterness and joy is our capacity to forgive. If you are refusing to forgive people, you are missing a wonderful opportunity of experiencing joy and sharing it with them.

CHECK IT OUT:

Psalm 103:12. *God has taken our sins far away.*
Ezekiel 36:25. *God cleanses us from sin.*
Joel 2:12-13. *Return to the Lord.*
Matthew 6:14-15. *Forgive others because God has forgiven you.*
Luke 3:3. *Turn from sin and God will forgive you.*
Acts 13:38-39. *Trust in Christ for forgiveness.*
Colossians 3:13. *Be ready to forgive others.*
Hebrews 9:22. *Jesus died so we could be forgiven.*
1 John 1:8-9. *Recognize sin and ask God to forgive you.*

(see also Confession and Repentance)

FRIENDSHIPS

Example of a Beautiful Friendship

Bible Reading: 1 Samuel 18:1-4; 20:12-17, 41-42; 23:16-18

Key Verse: *Jonathan made David swear again by his love for him; for he loved him as he loved his own life.* 1 Samuel 20:17, NRSV

When David and Jonathan met, they became close friends at once. Although Jonathan was probably somewhat older than David, their friendship is one of the deepest and closest recorded in the Bible because they (1) based their friendship on commitment to God, not just each other; (2) let nothing come between them, not even career or family problems; (3) drew closer together when their friendship was tested; and (4) were able to remain friends to the end.

Jonathan, the prince of Israel, later realized that David, and not he, would be king (23:17). But that did not weaken his love for David. Jonathan would much rather lose the throne of Israel than his closest friend. Their example of friendship is one we should follow. What would you be willing to sacrifice for your friends?

Faithful or Fickle?

Bible Reading: Psalm 55:1-23

Key Verses: *If an enemy were insulting me, I could endure it; if a foe were raising himself against me, I could hide from him. But it is you, a man like myself, my companion, my close friend.* Psalm 55:12-13, NIV

Nothing hurts as much as a wound from a friend. Real friends, however, stick by you in times of trouble and bring healing, love, acceptance, and understanding. There will be times when friends lovingly confront us, and their motives will be to help. A true friend speaks the truth, no matter how much it hurts to hear. What kind of friend are you? faithful or fickle? Don't betray those you love.

How to Be a True Friend

Bible Reading: Proverbs 18:24

Key Verse: *Some friends play at friendship but a true friend sticks closer than one's nearest kin.* Proverbs 18:24, NRSV

Loneliness is rampant. Many people today feel cut off and alienated from others. Being in a crowd just makes people more aware of their isolation. Lonely people don't need to hear, "Have a nice day." They need friends who will stick close, listen, care, and offer help when it is needed—in good times and bad. It is better to have one such friend than dozens of superficial acquaintances. Instead of wishing you could find a true friend, seek to become one yourself. There are people who need your friendship. Ask God to reveal them to you, and then take on the challenge of being a true friend.

What about Non-Christian Friends?

Bible Reading: 2 Corinthians 5:17-21; 6:14-18

Key Verse: *Do not be mismatched with unbelievers. For what partnership is there between righteousness and lawlessness? Or what fellowship is there between light and darkness?* 2 Corinthians 6:14, NRSV

It's no secret: Your closest friends affect the way you act. Consider the friends you hang around with. You probably do the same things, use the same slang, laugh at the same jokes, etc. If you have two sets of friends—your Christian friends and your non-Christian friends—it's easy to become a different person with each group.

Unfortunately, hanging around with friends who aren't Christians will not help you to become a stronger Christian. Most likely you'll tend to become like them and not grow closer to God.

However, God doesn't want you totally isolated from those who aren't Christians. In fact, if you get to the point where you don't have any non-Christian friends, you're probably doing something wrong. As a Christian, you should be Christ's representative to those who don't know him. To do that you have to be around them! Just be careful not to become like them, and remember that your goal is to point them to Christ.

CHECK IT OUT:

Genesis 14:14-16. *Friends help in times of trouble.*
Genesis 45:5. *Real friends forgive each other.*
Exodus 32:11-13. *Pray for your friends.*
2 Samuel 19:31-32. *Real friends stick with us during tough times.*
Psalm 1:1; Proverbs 13:20. *You'll become like those you spend time with.*

Proverbs 17:17. *Friends love in the good and bad times.*
Jeremiah 26:24. *Stand up for your friends.*
Daniel 3:16-18. *Godly friendships are powerful.*
John 15:13-15. *Jesus proved his friendship to us.*
Acts 9:23-29. *Barnabas was a true friend to Paul.*

(see also Peer Pressure and Popularity)

FUTURE

God Sees the Future

Bible Reading: Isaiah 41:1-10

Key Verse: *Who has performed and done this, calling the generations from the beginning?* Isaiah 41:4, NRSV

Each generation gets caught up in its own problems, but God's plan embraces all generations. When your great-grandparents lived, God worked personally in the lives of his people. When your great-grandchildren live, God will still work personally in the lives of his people. He is the only one who sees as clearly a hundred years from now as he saw a hundred years ago. When you are concerned about the future, talk with God, who knows the generations of the future as well as he knows the generations of the past.

Reading the Stars?

Bible Reading: Jeremiah 10:1-10

Key Verses: *This is what the LORD says: "Do not learn the ways of the nations or be terrified by signs in the sky, though the nations are terrified by them. For the customs of the peoples are worthless."* Jeremiah 10:2-3, NIV

Everyone would like to know the future. Decisions would be easier, failures avoided, and success assured. The people of Judah wanted to know the future too, and they tried to discern it in horoscopes. Jeremiah's response applies today: God made the stars that people consult. No one will discover the future in made-up charts of God's stars. But God, who promises to guide you, knows your future and will be with you all the way. He may not reveal your future to you, but he will walk with you as the future unfolds. Don't trust the stars. Trust the one who made the stars.

There Will Be an End

Bible Reading: Nahum 1:1-8

Key Verse: *The LORD is slow to anger and great in power, and the LORD will by no means leave the guilty unpunished.*
Nahum 1:3, NASB

God is slow to get angry, but when he is ready to punish, even the earth trembles. Often people avoid God because they see evildoers in the world and hypocrites in the church. They don't realize that because God is slow to anger, he gives his true followers time to share his love and truth with evildoers. But judgment will come. God will not allow sin to go unchecked forever. When people wonder why God doesn't punish evil immediately, remind them that if he did, none of us would be here. We can all be thankful that God gives people time to turn to him.

Jesus Will Return

Bible Reading: Zechariah 9:1-10; 12:3-4

Key Verse: *Behold, your King is coming to you; He is just and having salvation, lowly and riding on a donkey, a colt, the foal of a donkey.*   Zechariah 9:9, NKJV

The Triumphal Entry—when Jesus rode a colt into Jerusalem (Matthew 21:1-11)—was predicted here five hundred years before it happened. But just as this prophecy was fulfilled when Jesus came to earth, the prophecies of his second coming are just as certain to come true. We should be ready for his return, because he is coming! Are you ready for Christ's return? Are you living as you should? If not, start living for him today. Don't delay! His return is certain and coming soon.

Glorious Future

Bible Reading: 1 Corinthians 2:1-16

Key Verse: *Eye has not seen, nor ear heard, nor have entered into the heart of man the things which God has prepared for those who love Him.* 1 Corinthians 2:9, NKJV

We cannot imagine all God has in store for us both in this life and for eternity. He will create a new heaven and new earth (Isaiah 65:17; Revelation 21:1), and we will live with him forever. Until then, his Holy Spirit comforts and guides us. Knowing the future that awaits us should give us hope and courage to press on in this life, to endure hardship, and to avoid giving in to temptation. This world is not all there is.

Living While You Wait

Bible Reading: Revelation 10:1-11

Key Verse: *And when the seven thunders had sounded, I was about to write, but I heard a voice from heaven saying, "Seal up what the seven thunders have said, and do not write it down."* Revelation 10:4, NRSV

Throughout history people have wanted to know what would happen in the future, and God reveals some of it in this book. But John was stopped from revealing certain parts of his vision. An angel also told the prophet Daniel that some things he saw were not to be revealed yet to everyone (Daniel 12:9), and Jesus told his disciples that the time of the end is known only by God (Mark 13:32-33). God has revealed all we need to know to live for him now. In our desire to be ready for the end, we must not place more emphasis on speculation about the last days than on living godly lives while waiting.

CHECK IT OUT:

Genesis 12:1-4. *Your future is bright if you obey God.*
Exodus 3:18-22. *You can trust your future to God.*
Psalm 105:1-45. *We can be confident in the future.*
John 3:16. *Our future is in heaven.*
John 14:19-21. *Jesus will protect our future.*
2 Timothy 2:11-13. *Don't give up your future in heaven.*
Revelation 21–22. *Our future home will be wonderful.*

GOALS
(SEE ACHIEVEMENTS)

GOD'S WILL

Finding God's Will Requires Obedience

Bible Reading: Genesis 12:1-9

Key Verse: *I will make you a great nation; I will bless you and make your name great; and you shall be a blessing.*

Genesis 12:2, NKJV

God promised to bless Abram and make him great, but there was one condition. Abram had to do what God wanted him to do. This meant leaving his home and friends and traveling to a new land where God promised to build a great nation from Abram's family. Abram obeyed, leaving his home for God's promise of even greater blessings in the future. God may be trying to lead you to a place of greater service and usefulness for him. Don't let the comfort and security of your present position make you miss God's plan for you.

Not Qualified?

Bible Reading: Genesis 48:1-20

Key Verse: *But his father refused and said, "I know, my son, I know; he also shall become a people and he also shall be great. However, his younger brother shall be greater than he, and his descendants shall become a multitude of nations."* Genesis 48:19, NASB

Jacob gave Ephraim the greater blessing, instead of his older brother, Manasseh. When Joseph objected, Jacob refused to listen because God had told him that Ephraim would become greater. God often works in unexpected ways. When he chooses people to fulfill his plans, he always goes deeper than appearance, tradition, or position. He sometimes surprises us by choosing the less obvious person. God can use you to carry out his plans, even if you don't think you have all the qualifications.

Divine Appointments

Bible Reading: 1 Samuel 9:1-27

Key Verse: *So when Samuel saw Saul, the LORD said to him, "There he is, the man of whom I spoke to you. This one shall reign over My people."*   1 Samuel 9:17, NKJV

Often we think that events just happen to us, but as we learn from this story about Saul, God often uses common occurrences to lead us where he wants. It is important to evaluate all situations as potential "divine appointments" designed to shape our lives. Think of all the good and bad circumstances that have affected you lately. Can you see God's purpose in them? Perhaps he is building a certain quality in your life or leading you to serve him in a new area.

When God Says No

Bible Reading: 2 Samuel 7:1-16

Key Verses: *But that same night the word of the LORD came to Nathan: Go and tell my servant David: Thus says the LORD: Are you the one to build me a house to live in?*   2 Samuel 7:4-5, NRSV

David's request was good, but God said no. This does not mean that God rejected David. In fact, God was planning to do something even greater in David's life than allowing him the prestige of building the temple. Although God turned down David's request, he promised to continue the house (or dynasty) of David forever. David's earthly dynasty ended four centuries later, but Jesus Christ, a direct descendant of David, was the ultimate fulfillment of this promise (Acts 2:22-36). He will reign for eternity—first in his spiritual kingdom, and ultimately on earth in the new Jerusalem (Luke 1:30-33; Revelation 21). Have you prayed with good intentions only to have God say no? This is not rejection but God's way of fulfilling a greater purpose in your life.

God's Will Comes to Pass

Bible Reading: 2 Chronicles 18:9-34

Key Verse: *Now a certain man drew a bow at random, and struck the king of Israel between the joints of his armor. So he said to the driver of his chariot, "Turn around and take me out of the battle, for I am wounded."*

2 Chronicles 18:33, NKJV

Micaiah prophesied death for King Ahab, so Ahab disguised himself to fool the enemy. Apparently the disguise worked, but that didn't change the prophecy. A random Syrian arrow found a crack in his armor and killed him. God's will is always fulfilled despite the defenses people try to erect. God can use anything, even an error, to bring his will to pass. This is good news for God's followers, because we can trust him to work out his plans and keep his promises no matter what the circumstances.

Be Confident in God

Bible Reading: Habakkuk 3:15-19

Key Verse: *The LORD God is my strength; He will make my feet like deer's feet, and He will make me walk on my high hills.*

Habakkuk 3:19, NKJV

Habakkuk had asked God why evil people prosper while the righteous suffer. God's answer: They don't; not in the long run. Habakkuk saw his own limitations in contrast to God's unlimited control of all the world's events. God is alive and in control of the world and its events. We cannot see all that God is doing, and we cannot see all that God will do. But we can be assured that he is God and will do what is right. Knowing this brings us confidence and hope in the midst of a confusing world.

How to Seek God's Will

Bible Reading: Acts 16:1-12

Key Verse: *They went through the region of Phrygia and Galatia, having been forbidden by the Holy Spirit to speak the word in Asia.*   Acts 16:6, NRSV

We don't know how the Holy Spirit told Paul that he and his men were not to go into Asia. It may have been through a prophet, a vision, an inner conviction, or some other circumstance. To know God's will does not mean we must hear his voice. He leads in different ways. When seeking God's will, (1) make sure your plan is in harmony with God's Word; (2) ask mature Christians for their advice; (3) check your own motives (are you trying to do what you want or what you think God wants?); and (4) pray for God to open and close the doors of circumstances.

God's Will vs. My Will

Bible Reading: Ephesians 2:1-12; 5:15-18

Key Verse: *For we are God's workmanship, created in Christ Jesus to do good works, which God prepared in advance for us to do.*   Ephesians 2:10, NIV

Every person has a will, a part of the brain that is the "chooser." God has allowed us to use our will to sometimes go against his will, which is the essence of sin. It isn't God's will for us to sin. While God is strong enough to force his will on us, he doesn't do that. Because he loves us, he allows us to make choices. God doesn't force us to follow him; he wants us to follow him because we want to. Unfortunately, many people use their will to reject Christ and his will for their lives.

Christians, however, should desire to do God's will. But what *is* God's will for us? First, he wants us to know him. Second, he wants us to help others. Third, he wants us to be filled with the Holy Spirit. By allowing God to fill you, you are really saying, "God, take my will and help me to do your will."

CHECK IT OUT:

Genesis 19:31-36. *Don't let your will supersede God's will.*

Psalm 16:7-8. *God's will guides you.*

Jeremiah 29:11-13. *God's plans are good.*

Micah 6:8. *God has revealed what he desires.*

Matthew 1:18-25. *Follow God's will even if you don't understand it.*

Philippians 2:13-16. *God wants to help you do his will.*

(see also Bible, Guidance, and Obedience)

GOSSIP

Don't Pass It On

Bible Reading: Exodus 23:1-13

Key Verse: *You shall not circulate a false report. Do not put your hand with the wicked to be an unrighteous witness.*

Exodus 23:1, NKJV

Making up or passing along untrue reports was strictly forbidden by God. Gossip, slander, and false witnessing undermined families, strained neighborhood cooperation, and made chaos of the justice system. Destructive gossip still causes problems. Even if you do not initiate a lie, you become responsible if you pass it along. Don't circulate rumors—squelch them.

Gossip Hurts

Bible Reading: Proverbs 25:15-28

Key Verse: *Like a club and a sword and a sharp arrow is a man who bears false witness against his neighbor.*

Proverbs 25:18, NASB

Lying is vicious. Its effects can be as permanent as those of a stab wound. The next time you are tempted to pass on a bit of gossip, imagine yourself striking the victim of your remarks with an axe. This image may shock you into silence.

CHECK IT OUT:

Leviticus 19:16. *God says not to gossip.*

Psalm 57:4-11. *When others gossip about you, praise God instead of gossiping about them.*

Psalm 141:3. *Keep your mouth shut when needed.*

Proverbs 11:13. *A gossip spreads rumors.*

Proverbs 16:28. *A gossip separates friends.*

Proverbs 26:20, 22. *Gossip causes tension.*

Romans 1:29. *Evil people are full of gossip.*

2 Thessalonians 3:11-12. *God hates gossiping.*

1 Timothy 5:13. *Gossipers should learn to be quiet.*

Titus 3:2. *Don't speak unkindly of anyone.*

James 3:1-16. *Control your tongue.*

GUIDANCE

The Long Way Around

Bible Reading: Exodus 13:17-22

Key Verse: *When Pharaoh let the people go, God did not lead them on the road through the Philistine country, though that was shorter. For God said, "If they face war, they might change their minds and return to Egypt."*

Exodus 13:17, NIV

God doesn't always work in the way that seems best to us. Instead of guiding the Israelites along the direct route from Egypt to the Promised Land, he took them by a longer route to avoid fighting with the Philistines. If God does not lead you along the shortest path to your goal, don't complain or resist. Follow him willingly and trust him to lead you safely around unseen obstacles. He can see the end of your journey from the beginning, and he knows the safest and best route.

Right Now

Bible Reading: Numbers 9:15-23

Key Verse: *At the command of the LORD they camped, and at the command of the LORD they set out; they kept the LORD's*

charge, according to the command of the LORD
through Moses.   Numbers 9:23, NASB

The Hebrews traveled and camped as God guided.
When you follow God's guidance, you know you are
where God wants you, whether you're moving or staying in one place. You are physically somewhere right
now. Instead of praying, "God, what do you want me
to do next?" ask, "God, what do you want me to do
while I'm right here?" Direction from God is not just
for your next big move. He has a purpose in placing
you where you are right now. Begin to understand
God's purpose for your life by discovering what he
wants you to do now!

Get Guidance First

Bible Reading: 1 Samuel 23:1-5

Key Verse: *David inquired of the* LORD, *"Shall I go and attack these*
Philistines?" The LORD *said to David, "Go and attack the*
Philistines and save Keilah."   1 Samuel 23:2, NRSV

David sought the Lord's guidance *before* he took action.
He listened to God's directions and then proceeded
accordingly. Rather than trying to find God's will *after*
the fact or having to ask God to undo the results of our
hasty decisions, we should take time to discern God's
will beforehand. We can hear him speak through the
counsel of others, his Word, and the leading of his Spirit
in our hearts, as well as through circumstances.

Constant Reliance

Bible Reading: Psalm 27:1-14

Key Verse: *For he will hide me in his shelter in the day of trouble; he*
will conceal me under the cover of his tent; he will set me
high on a rock.   Psalm 27:5, NRSV

We often run to God when we are experiencing difficulties. But David sought God's guiding presence *every day*.
When troubles came his way, he was *already* in God's
presence and prepared to handle any test. Believers can
call to God for help at any time, but how shortsighted to

call on God only after trouble has come. Many of our problems could be avoided or handled far more easily by relying on God's help and direction every day.

The Bible, God's Map

Bible Reading: Psalm 48:1-14

Key Verse: *For this God is our God for ever and ever; he will be our guide even to the end.* Psalm 48:14, NIV

We often pray for God's guidance as we struggle with decisions. What we need is both guidance and a guide—a map that gives us landmarks and directions, and a constant companion who has an intimate knowledge of the way and will make sure we interpret the map correctly. The Bible is just such a map, and God is our constant companion and guide. As you make your way through life, lean upon both the map and the Guide.

CHECK IT OUT:

Exodus 4:1-17. *God supplies all your needs.*
Deuteronomy 4:19; 17:2-5. *Don't look to astrology, not even in fun.*
Psalm 25:4-7. *Pray for God to lead you.*
Proverbs 14:7. *Don't get advice from fools.*
Proverbs 16:9. *Make plans, but let God direct you and change them.*
Jeremiah 10:2. *Horoscopes are worthless.*
Matthew 2:13-15. *If your heart is open, God can lead you.*
Acts 8:26-37. *God's guidance leads to blessing.*

(see also God's Will)

GUILT

Turn Back to God

Bible Reading: Judges 16:23-31

Key Verse: *Then Samson called to the LORD, saying, "O Lord GOD, remember me, I pray! Strengthen me, I pray, just this*

once, O God, that I may with one blow take vengeance
on the Philistines for my two eyes!"   Judges 16:28, NKJV

In spite of Samson's past, God still answered his prayer
and destroyed the heathen temple and worshipers. God
still loved Samson. He was willing to hear Samson's
prayer of confession and repentance and use him this
final time. One of the effects of sin in our lives is to keep
us from feeling like praying. But perfect moral behavior
is not a condition for prayer. Don't let guilt feelings over
sin keep you apart from God. No matter how long you
have been away from God, he is ready to hear from you
and restore you to a right relationship. Every situation
can be salvaged if you are willing to turn to him again. If
God still could work in Samson's situation, he can certainly make something worthwhile out of yours.

Not beyond Forgiveness

Bible Reading: 2 Chronicles 33:1-19

Key Verse: *While he was in distress he entreated the favor of the*
LORD his God and humbled himself greatly before the
God of his ancestors.   2 Chronicles 33:12, NRSV

In a list of corrupt kings, Manasseh would rank near the
top. His life is a catalog of evil deeds including idol worship, sacrificing his own children, and temple desecra-
tion. Eventually, however, he realized his sins and cried
out to God for forgiveness, and God listened. If God can
forgive Manasseh, surely he can forgive anyone. Are
you burdened by overpowering guilt? Do you doubt
that anyone could forgive what you have done? Take
heart—until death, no one is beyond God's forgiveness.

Good Enough?

Bible Reading: Hebrews 9:9-15

Key Verse: *For this reason Christ is the mediator of a new covenant,*
that those who are called may receive the promised
eternal inheritance—now that he has died as a ransom
to set them free from the sins committed under the first
covenant.   Hebrews 9:15, NIV

Though you know Christ, you may still be trying to make yourself good enough for God. But rules and rituals have never cleansed people's hearts. By Jesus' blood alone (1) our consciences are cleared, (2) we are freed from death and can live to serve God, and (3) we are freed from sin's power. If you are carrying a load of guilt because you can't be good enough for God, take another look at Jesus' death and what it means for you.

Why Do I Keep On Sinning?

Bible Reading: James 4:7-17

Key Verse: *Anyone, then, who knows the right thing to do and fails to do it, commits sin.* James 4:17, NRSV

When you accepted Christ as Savior, God declared you "not guilty" of all your sins. All those bad things you did (or the good things you didn't do) in the past were forgiven. But being forgiven doesn't mean you stop sinning. You must deal with sin daily while you're still alive on earth. It's part of being human.

Christ has wiped away all our past sins, but what about our present sins? God has forgiven us for these too, but we confess them to him to keep the communication channels open and to keep the relationship close. One of the roles of the Holy Spirit is to remind us when we sin. He doesn't do this to condemn us, but to prompt us to confess it, forsake it, and move on. So we should talk to God about our lives, and confess, whenever we need to. Remember, sins aren't limited to doing what is wrong. They also include not doing what is right.

Let God do the convicting in your life, and then confess your sins to him. He's eager to clear away the barriers between you and himself and start fresh.

Christ Removes Your Guilt

Bible Reading: Revelation 7:1-17

Key Verse: *They cried out in a loud voice, saying, "Salvation belongs to our God who is seated on the throne, and to the Lamb!"* Revelation 7:10, NRSV

People try many methods to remove the guilt of sin—good works, intellectual pursuits, and even placing blame. The crowd in heaven, however, praises God, saying, "Salvation belongs to our God who is seated on the throne, and to the Lamb." Salvation from sin's penalty can come only through Jesus Christ. Have you had the guilt of your sin removed in the only way possible?

CHECK IT OUT:

Genesis 3:7-11. *Guilt tells us when we sin.*
Matthew 27:23-26. *Pilate couldn't wash away guilt.*
Romans 3:9-12. *Everyone is guilty of sin.*
1 Timothy 1:12-17. *Thank God that he wipes away guilt.*

(see also Confession and Forgiveness)

HOLY SPIRIT

The Holy Spirit in the Old Testament

Bible Reading: 1 Chronicles 12:8-18

Key Verse: *Then the Spirit came upon Amasai, chief of the Thirty, and he said: "We are yours, O David!"*

1 Chronicles 12:18, NIV

How did the Holy Spirit work in Old Testament times? When there was an important job to be done, God chose a person to do it, and the Spirit gave that person the needed power and ability. The Spirit gave Bezalel artistic ability (Exodus 31:1-5), Jephthah military prowess (Judges 11:29), David power to rule (1 Samuel 16:13), and Zechariah an authoritative word of prophecy (2 Chronicles 24:20). Here the Holy Spirit came upon David's warriors. Beginning at Pentecost, however, the Spirit came upon all believers (Acts 2:14-21). That same Spirit is ready to equip you.

Power to Witness

Bible Reading: Micah 3:1-8

Key Verse: *But truly I am full of power by the Spirit of the LORD, and of justice and might, to declare to Jacob his transgression and to Israel his sin.* Micah 3:8, NKJV

Micah attributed the power of his ministry to God's Spirit. Our power comes from the same source. Jesus told his followers they would receive power to witness about him when the Holy Spirit came to them (Acts 1:8). You can't witness effectively by relying on your own strength because fear will keep you from speaking out for God. Only by relying on the power of the Holy Spirit can you live and witness for him.

Ability to Understand

Bible Reading: Luke 24:35-49

Key Verse: *Then he opened their minds so they could understand the Scriptures.* Luke 24:45, NIV

Jesus opened these people's minds to understand the Scriptures. The Holy Spirit does this in our lives today when we study the Bible. Have you ever wondered how to understand a difficult Bible passage? Besides reading surrounding passages, asking other people, and consulting reference works, pray that the Holy Spirit will open your mind to understand, giving you the needed insight to put God's Word into action in your life.

Who Is the Holy Spirit?

Bible Reading: John 3:1-16

Key Verse: *That which is born of the flesh is flesh, and that which is born of the Spirit is spirit.* John 3:6, NKJV

The Holy Spirit is the third person in the Trinity—God the Father being the first and Jesus, his Son, being the second. In Old Testament days the Holy Spirit empowered specific individuals only for specific purposes. But after Jesus physically ascended into heaven, he sent his spiritual presence—the Holy Spirit—to all believers so that he would still be among mankind (see Luke 24:49). The Holy Spirit first became available to all believers at Pentecost (Acts 2:1-4).

The Comforter

Bible Reading: John 16:1-16

Key Verse: *But I tell you the truth, it is to your advantage that I go away; for if I do not go away, the Helper shall not come to you; but if I go, I will send Him to you.* John 16:7, NASB

In his last moments with his disciples, Jesus (1) warned them about further persecution; (2) told them where he was going, when he was leaving, and why; and (3) assured them they would not be left alone but that the Spirit would come. He knew what lay ahead, and he did

not want their faith shaken or destroyed. God wants
you to know that you are not alone in the world. You
have the Holy Spirit to comfort you, teach you truth,
and help you.

CHECK IT OUT:

Judges 3:10. *The Holy Spirit makes people clean and strong.*
Matthew 12:31-32. *Never sin against the Holy Spirit.*
John 3:5-8. *The Holy Spirit gives new life.*
John 14:15-21. *The Holy Spirit lives in us.*
John 15:26. *The Holy Spirit testifies to the truth about Jesus.*
John 16:8. *The Holy Spirit convicts us of sin.*
Romans 8:2, 9-11. *The Holy Spirit helps us live as
    Christians and is present in all Christians.*
1 Corinthians 12:4-13. *The Holy Spirit gives spiritual
    gifts that build up the body of Christ.*
2 Corinthians 1:22. *The Holy Spirit guarantees that we
    belong to God.*
2 Corinthians 5:16-17. *The Holy Spirit makes us new people.*
Galatians 5:22-25. *The Holy Spirit bears fruit in our life.*

HOMOSEXUALITY

A Bad Alternative

Bible Reading: Romans 1:16-32

Key Verses: *For this reason God gave them up to degrading passions.
Their women exchanged natural intercourse for
unnatural, and in the same way also the men, giving up
natural intercourse with women, were consumed with
passion for one another.* Romans 1:26-27, NRSV

Paul clearly wrote to the Romans that all people every-
where are without excuse in knowing that there is a
Creator—God himself. Paul has harsh words for those
who deny God and his plan for creation, especially in
the forms of idolatry and homosexuality.

Christians need to understand two important messages
from God regarding homosexuality. First, homosexuality
is *not* an acceptable alternate lifestyle. It is wrong, and it is
sinful. Second, homosexuality is a behavior that *can* be

forgiven and changed with God's help. Jesus' death on the cross paid for the sin of homosexuality, just as it paid for the sins of lying, lust, hate, and pride. Homosexuals, like all sinners, stand guilty before God. But there is hope for sinners of all kinds through the life, death, and resurrection of Jesus Christ. He is the one who will set us free, regardless of our sin.

CHECK IT OUT:

Leviticus 18:22. *God forbids homosexual relationships.*
Leviticus 18:29. *There is a penalty for homosexual sin.*
1 Kings 14:24. *Homosexual practices are an abomination.*
Matthew 7:1. *Pray for and witness to homosexuals.*

HONESTY

Afraid of Getting Caught?

Bible Reading: Genesis 27:1-13
Key Verses: *Jacob said to Rebekah his mother, "But my brother Esau is a hairy man, and I'm a man with smooth skin. What if my father touches me? I would appear to be tricking him and would bring down a curse on myself rather than a blessing."* Genesis 27:11-12, NIV

How we react to a moral dilemma often exposes our real motives. Frequently we are more worried about getting caught than about doing what is right. Jacob did not seem concerned about the deceitfulness of his mother's plan. Instead, he was afraid of getting in trouble while carrying it out. If you are worried about getting caught, you are probably in a position that is less than honest. Let your fear of getting caught be a warning to do right. Jacob paid a huge price for carrying out this dishonest plan. Don't follow his example.

Keeping Your Word

Bible Reading: Joshua 14:6-15
Key Verse: *Then Joshua blessed him, and gave Hebron to Caleb son of Jephunneh for an inheritance.* Joshua 14:13, NRSV

When Joshua gave Caleb his land, he fulfilled a promise God had made to Caleb forty-five years earlier. We expect such integrity and reliability from God, but do we expect the same from his followers? How about you? Is your word this reliable? Would you honor a forty-five-year-old promise? God would—and does. Even today he is honoring promises he made *thousands* of years ago. In fact, some of his greatest promises are yet to be fulfilled. This gives us much to look forward to. Let your faith grow as you realize how God keeps his word.

Actions Speak Louder

Bible Reading: Ezekiel 23:36-45

Key Verse: *For when they had slaughtered their children for their idols, on the same day they came into my sanctuary to profane it. This is what they did in my house.*

Ezekiel 23:39, NRSV

The Israelites went so far as to sacrifice their own children to idols and then sacrifice to the Lord the same day. This made a mockery of worship. We cannot praise God and willfully sin at the same time! That would be like agreeing to go steady with one person, then going on a date with someone else. You have to do more than just say the words—you must show what you really believe and value by your actions.

An Honest Worker

Bible Reading: Ezekiel 45:9-12

Key Verse: *"Enough, O princes of Israel! Remove violence and plundering, execute justice and righteousness, and stop dispossessing My people," says the Lord* GOD.

Ezekiel 45:9, NKJV

Greed and extortion were two of the major social sins of the nation during this time (see Amos 5:7-13). In the new economy there would be plenty of land for the "princes" (45:7-8) and no longer any basis for greed. Therefore, the princes and the people were commanded to be fair and honest, especially when they did business. Consider the ways you measure goods, money, or services. If you are paid for an hour of work, be sure you work for a full hour. If you sell a bushel of apples, make sure it is a full bushel. God is completely trustworthy, and his followers should be, too.

CHECK IT OUT:

Genesis 29:28-30. *Keep your end of a bargain.*

Joshua 7:7-12. *Be honest in your prayers.*

Psalm 24:1-6. *Only honest people may stand before the Lord.*

Proverbs 19:1. *It is better to be honest and poor than dishonest and rich.*

Isaiah 33:15-16. *Living honestly is important in your relationship with God.*

Micah 7:1-4. *Honest people are hard to find.*

Matthew 5:33-37. *Your word is your honor.*

John 13:37-38. *Be honest in your evaluation of yourself.*

1 Thessalonians 2:4-5. *Be honest in witnessing.*

Titus 1:5-8; 2:11–3:8. *Christian leaders must have integrity.*

James 5:12. *Don't swear, lie, or exaggerate.*

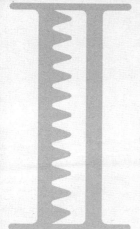

INTEGRITY
(SEE HONESTY)

JEALOUSY

Jealousy's Dangers

Bible Reading: Genesis 26:12-25

Key Verse: *He had so many flocks and herds and servants that the Philistines envied him.*   Genesis 26:14, NIV

God kept his promise to bless Isaac. Because of God's blessing, everything Isaac did seemed to go right, and the neighboring Philistines became jealous. So they plugged his wells and tried to get rid of him. Jealousy is a dividing force strong enough to tear apart the mightiest of nations or the closest of friends. When you find yourself becoming jealous of others, try thanking God for their good fortune. Before striking out in anger, consider what you could lose.

Are You Keeping Score?

Bible Reading: Genesis 37:1-28

Key Verses: *And they said to one another, "Here comes this dreamer! Now then, come and let us kill him and throw him into one of the pits; and we will say, 'A wild beast devoured him.' Then let us see what will become of his dreams!"*
Genesis 37:19-20, NASB

Could jealousy ever make you feel like killing someone? Before saying, "Of course not," look at what happened in this story. Ten men were willing to kill their younger brother over a cloak and a few reported dreams. Their deep jealousy had grown into ugly rage, blinding them completely to what was right. Jealousy can be hard to recognize because our reasons for it seem to make sense. But left unchecked, jealousy grows quickly and leads to serious sins. The longer you cultivate jealous feelings, the harder it is to uproot them. The time to deal with jealousy is when you notice yourself keeping score of what others have.

Don't Let It Hinder God's Work

Bible Reading: Acts 13:42-52

Key Verse: *When the Jews saw the crowds, they were filled with jealousy and talked abusively against what Paul was saying.* Acts 13:45, NIV

The Jewish leaders brought theological arguments against Paul and Barnabas, but the Bible tells us that the real reason for their denunciation was jealousy (5:17). When we see others succeeding where we haven't or receiving the glory that we want, it is hard to be happy for them. Jealousy is our natural reaction. But it is tragic when our own jealous feelings make us try to stop God's work. If a work is of God, rejoice in it—no matter who is doing it.

Encouragement, Not Jealousy

Bible Reading: 1 Corinthians 12:4-21

Key Verse: *And there are varieties of effects, but the same God who works all things in all persons.*
1 Corinthians 12:6, NASB

Using the analogy of the body, Paul emphasizes the importance of each church member. If a seemingly insignificant part is taken away, the whole body becomes less effective. Thinking that your gift is more important than someone else's is spiritual pride. We should not look down on those who seem unimportant, and we should not be jealous of others who have impressive gifts. Instead, we must use the gifts we have been given and encourage others to use theirs. If we don't, the body of believers will be less effective.

CHECK IT OUT:

Genesis 4:1-8. *Jealousy can lead to murder.*
Proverbs 14:30. *Jealousy can ruin your life.*
Proverbs 27:4. *Jealousy is dangerous.*

Matthew 18:1-6; Galatians 6:4. *Don't compare yourself with others.*

John 3:26-30. *Christ can remove all jealousy.*

Romans 13:11-14. *Jealousy can lead to many dangers.*

James 3:14-16. *Jealousy is not God's way.*

LEADERSHIP

Qualities of Good Leaders

Bible Reading: Deuteronomy 1:9-18

Key Verse: *Choose for each of your tribes individuals who are wise, discerning, and reputable to be your leaders.*
Deuteronomy 1:13, NRSV

Moses identified some of the inner qualities of good leaders: (1) fairness, (2) impartiality, (3) character strength, and (4) the ability to recognize their limitations. These characteristics differ greatly from the ones that often help elect leaders today: good looks, wealth, popularity, and a willingness to do anything to get to the top. The qualities Moses identified should be evident in our lives as we lead, and we should look for them in the lives of those we elect to positions of leadership.

Priorities of Good Leaders

Bible Reading: Judges 9:7-20

Key Verse: *If then you have acted in truth and sincerity with Jerubbaal and with his house this day, then rejoice in Abimelech, and let him also rejoice in you.* Judges 9:19, NKJV

Jotham told the story about the trees in order to help the people set good priorities. He did not want them to appoint a leader of low character. As we serve in leadership positions, we should examine our motives. Do we just want praise, prestige, or power? In the parable, the good trees chose to be productive and to provide benefits to people. If you want to be a leader, make sure these are your priorities.

Accountable to God

Bible Reading: 2 Chronicles 19:1-11

Key Verse: *Now then let the fear of the LORD be upon you; be very*

careful what you do, for the LORD our God will have no part in unrighteousness, or partiality, or the taking of a bribe.   2 Chronicles 19:7, NASB

Jehoshaphat delegated some of the responsibilities for ruling and judging the people, but he warned his appointees that they were accountable to God for the standards they used to judge others. Jehoshaphat's advice is helpful for all leaders: (1) Allow God to help you be just; (2) be impartial; (3) be honest; and (4) act only out of fear of God, not people.

Effective Leadership

Bible Reading: Nehemiah 2:9-20

Key Verse: *And I told them of the hand of my God which had been good upon me, and also of the king's words that he had spoken to me. So they said, "Let us rise up and build." Then they set their hands to this good work.*   Nehemiah 2:18, NKJV

Nehemiah's life story provides many principles of effective leadership that are still valid today: (1) *Have a clear purpose,* and keep evaluating it in light of God's will. Nothing prevented Nehemiah from staying on track. (2) *Be straightforward and honest.* Everyone knew exactly what Nehemiah needed, and he spoke the truth even when it made his goal harder to achieve. (3) *Live above reproach.* The accusations against Nehemiah were empty and false. (4) *Be a person of constant prayer,* deriving power and wisdom from your contact with God. Everything Nehemiah did glorified God.

Leadership appears glamorous at times, but it is often lonely, thankless, and filled with pressures to compromise values and standards. Nehemiah was able to accomplish a huge task against incredible odds because he learned that there is no success without risk of failure, no reward without hard work, no opportunity without criticism, and no true leadership without trust in God.

CHECK IT OUT:

Exodus 2:11–3:10. *God prepared Moses for leadership.*
1 Chronicles 21:7-8. *Leaders must accept responsibility.*
Proverbs 11:14. *Nations need wise leaders.*

Jeremiah 17:7-8. *Let the Lord be your leader.*
Matthew 12:19-21. *Qualities of good leaders.*
Matthew 20:26-28. *Leaders must be servants.*
2 Timothy 1:7. *Qualifications of a good leader.*
Hebrews 12:2. *Keep your eyes on Christ, your leader.*

LIFESTYLE

What Kind of Ambassador Are You?

Bible Reading: Exodus 7:1-7

Key Verse: *The LORD said to Moses, "See, I have made you like God to Pharaoh, and your brother Aaron shall be your prophet.*
Exodus 7:1, NRSV

God called Moses his ambassador. An ambassador represents another country, another type of people, and often another point of view. Each of us is God's ambassador—representing his values and character to the world. Much of the world knows nothing about God except what it sees in the lives of his people. What kind of god would they think you represent? Take note of how your actions and lifestyle come across to others. It's a good indication of how well you are representing God.

God Wants Holiness

Bible Reading: Leviticus 11:39-47

Key Verse: *I am the LORD who brought you up out of Egypt to be your God; therefore be holy, because I am holy.*
Leviticus 11:45, NIV

These verses provide a key to understanding all the laws and regulations in Leviticus. God wanted his people to be *holy* (set apart, different, unique), just as he is holy. He knew they had only two options: to be separate and holy, or to compromise with their heathen neighbors and become corrupt. That is why he called them out of idolatrous Egypt and set them apart as a unique nation, dedicated to worshiping him alone and leading moral lives. That is also why he designed laws and restrictions to help them remain separate—both socially and spiritually—from the wicked heathen nations they would encounter in Canaan.

Like the Israelites, Christians also are called to be holy (1 Peter 1:15). We are to remain spiritually separate from the world's wickedness, even though we rub shoulders with unbelievers every day. It is no easy task to be holy in an unholy world, but God doesn't ask you to accomplish this on your own. Through the death of his Son, he will present you holy and blameless before him (Colossians 1:22).

Live It!

Bible Reading: Jeremiah 23:25-32

Key Verse: *"The prophet who has a dream may relate his dream, but let him who has My word speak My word in truth. What does straw have in common with grain?" declares the* LORD.　　　　　　　　　　Jeremiah 23:28, NASB

True prophets and false prophets are as different as chaff and wheat. Worthless chaff blows away with the wind, while wheat remains to nourish many. To share God's Word is a great responsibility because the way we present it and live it will encourage people either to accept it or reject it. Whether we speak from a pulpit, teach in a class, or share with friends, we are entrusted with accurately communicating and living out God's Word. As you share God's Word with friends and neighbors, they will look for its effectiveness in your life. Unless it has changed you, why should they let it change them? If you want to share your faith in God, you'd better live it first!

Show Love

Bible Reading: Mark 12:28-34

Key Verse: *Love the Lord your God with all your heart and with all your soul and with all your mind and with all your strength.*　　　　　　　　　Mark 12:30, NIV

God's laws are not burdensome in number or detail. They can be reduced to two simple rules for life: Love God and love others. These commands are from the Old Testament (Leviticus 19:18; Deuteronomy 6:5). When you love God completely and care for others as you care for yourself, then you have fulfilled the intent of the Ten Command- ments and the other Old Testament laws. Let them rule your thoughts, decisions, and actions. When you are uncertain about what to do, ask yourself which course of action best demonstrates love for God and love for others.

Are You Denying Christ?

Bible Reading: Mark 14:10-11, 17-21

Key Verse: *Then Judas Iscariot, one of the Twelve, went to the chief priests to betray Jesus to them.* Mark 14:10, NIV

Judas, the very man who would betray Jesus, was at the table with the others. He had already determined to betray Jesus, but in cold-blooded hypocrisy he shared the fellowship of this meal. It is easy to become enraged or shocked by what Judas did, yet when we profess com- mitment to Christ and then deny him with our lives, we also betray him. We deny Christ's truth by living con- trary to how he taught us to live. We deny Christ's love by not obeying him, and we deny Christ's deity by rejecting his authority. Do your words and actions match? If not, consider a change of mind and heart that will protect you from making a terrible mistake.

What Changed When I Became a Christian?

Bible Reading: Colossians 1:1-14

Key Verse: *All over the world this gospel is bearing fruit and growing, just as it has been doing among you since the day you heard it and understood God's grace in all its truth.* Colossians 1:6, NIV

Wherever Paul went, he preached the gospel—to Gen- tile audiences, to hostile Jewish leaders, and even to his Roman guards. Whenever people believed in the mes- sage he spoke, they were changed. Becoming a Chris- tian transforms your life! Becoming a Christian means beginning a whole new relationship with God, not just turning over a new leaf or determining to do right. New believers have a changed purpose, direction, attitude, and behavior. They no longer seek to serve themselves but to serve God. In what areas has becoming a Christian changed your life? Where should it do so?

Saved to Serve

Bible Reading: 2 Peter 1:2-9

Key Verse: *To knowledge [add] self-control, to self-control perseverance, to perseverance godliness.* 2 Peter 1:6, NKJV

False teachers were saying that self-control was not needed because works do not help the believer anyway (2:19). It is true that works cannot save us, but it is absolutely false to think they are unimportant. We are saved so that we can grow to resemble Christ and so that we can serve others. God wants to produce his character in us. But to do this, he demands effort from us. To grow spiritually, we must develop self-control.

CHECK IT OUT:

Leviticus 10:1-7. *Live a life of obedience to God's commands.*
Jeremiah 18:18. *Lifestyle is determined by your beliefs.*
Matthew 12:33-37. *Your heart determines your words and lifestyle.*
1 Corinthians 6:20. *Live to give glory to God.*
Philippians 1:12-14. *Live for Christ.*
2 Timothy 3:1-9. *Being a Christian can be tough.*
1 Peter 4:10. *Have a serving lifestyle.*

(see also Attitudes and Christian Life)

LOVE

Love vs. Lust

Bible Reading: 2 Samuel 13:1-20

Key Verse: *Then Amnon was seized with a very great loathing for her; indeed, his loathing was even greater than the lust he had felt for her.* 2 Samuel 13:15, NRSV

Love and lust are very different. After Amnon raped his half sister, his "love" turned to hate. Although he had claimed to be in love, he was actually overcome by lust. Love is patient, while lust requires immediate sexual satisfaction. Love is kind, while lust is harsh. Love does not demand its own way, while lust does. You can read about the characteristics of real love in 1 Corinthians 13.

God's Love Is Changeless

Bible Reading: Psalm 59:1-17

Key Verse: *My God in his steadfast love will meet me; my God will let me look in triumph on my enemies.* Psalm 59:10, NRSV

David was hunted by those whose love had turned to jealousy, which was driving them to murder him. Trusted friends, and even his son, had turned against him. What changeable love! But David knew that God's love for him was *changeless.* God's love for all who trust him is also changeless. When the love of others fails or disappoints us, we can rest in God's changeless love.

Love Your Enemies

Bible Reading: Luke 6:20-38

Key Verse: *But I say to you who hear: Love your enemies, do good to those who hate you.* Luke 6:27, NKJV

The Jews despised the Romans because they oppressed God's people, but Jesus told them to love these enemies. Such words turned many away from Christ. But Jesus wasn't talking about having affection for enemies—he was talking about an act of the will. You can't "fall into" this kind of love—it takes conscious effort. Loving our enemies means acting in their best interests. We can pray for them, and we can think of ways to help them. Jesus loved the whole world, even though the world was in rebellion against God. He asks us to follow his example by loving our enemies.

Active Love

Bible Reading: John 13:31-35

Key Verse: *By this all men will know that you are my disciples, if you love one another.* John 13:35, NIV

Love is not simply warm feelings—it is instead an attitude that reveals itself in action. How can we love others as Christ loves us? By helping when it's not convenient, by giving when it hurts, by devoting energy to others' welfare rather than our own, by absorbing hurts from others without complaining or fighting back. This kind of loving is hard to do. That is why people will notice when you do it and will know you are empowered by a supernatural source.

True Love

Bible Reading: 1 Corinthians 13:1-13

Key Verse: *And now these three remain: faith, hope and love. But the greatest of these is love.* 1 Corinthians 13:13, NIV

Our society confuses love and lust. Unlike lust, God's kind of love is directed outward toward others, not inward toward ourselves. It is utterly unselfish. Love is as strong as death. It cannot be killed by time or disaster, and, since it is priceless, it cannot be bought for any price, because it is freely given.

Building Others Up

Bible Reading: James 4:1-12

Key Verse: *Do not speak evil against one another, brothers and sisters. Whoever speaks evil against another or judges another, speaks evil against the law and judges the law; but if you judge the law, you are not a doer of the law but a judge.* James 4:11, NRSV

Jesus summarized the entire law as loving God and neighbor (Matthew 22:37-40), and Paul said that love demonstrated toward a neighbor fully satisfies the law (Romans 13:6-10). When we fail to love, we are actually breaking God's law. Examine your attitude and actions toward others. Do you build people up or tear them down? When you're ready to criticize someone, remember God's law of love and say something good about him or her instead. If you make this a habit, your tendency to find fault with others will decrease and your ability to obey God's law will increase.

Love Is a Choice

Bible Reading: 1 John 2:3-21; 4:20-21

Key Verse: *Whoever loves a brother or sister lives in the light, and in such a person there is no cause for stumbling.*

1 John 2:10, NRSV

These verses are not talking about disliking a disagreeable Christian brother. There will always be people we will not like as well as others. John's words focus on the attitude that causes us to ignore or despise others, to treat them as irritants, competitors, or enemies. Fortunately, Christian love is not a feeling but a choice. We can choose to be concerned with people's well-being and to treat them with respect, whether or not we feel affection toward them. If we choose to love others, God will give us the necessary strength and will show us how to express our love.

We should remember that we cannot truly love God while neglecting to love those who are created in his image.

CHECK IT OUT:

Matthew 5:38-42. *Christlike love serves others.*
Matthew 5:43-48. *Love your enemies.*
Matthew 23:37-39. *Jesus shows how to love lost people.*
Romans 8:35-39. *Nothing can take God's love from us.*
Romans 12:9-21. *Love demands that we give of ourselves.*
Romans 13:10. *Love is the only law you need.*
Ephesians 3:17-19. *God's love is great.*
Colossians 3:14. *Let love guide your life.*
1 Peter 4:8. *Show deep love for other believers.*

LYING

Great Consequences

Bible Reading: Genesis 18:1-15

Key Verse: *Sarah was afraid, so she lied and said, "I did not laugh." But he said, "Yes, you did laugh."* Genesis 18:15, NIV

Sarah lied because she was afraid of being discovered. Fear is the most common motive for lying. When we lie, we are afraid that our inner thoughts and emotions will be exposed or our wrongdoings discovered. But lying causes greater complications than telling the truth and brings even more problems. In the long run, it's always better to tell the truth. Learn a lesson from Sarah, and be honest with others—especially God.

If God Is Not in It . . .

Bible Reading: 1 Samuel 15:1-26

Key Verse: *But Samuel replied: "Does the LORD delight in burnt offerings and sacrifices as much as in obeying the voice of the LORD? To obey is better than sacrifice, and to heed is better than the fat of rams."* 1 Samuel 15:22, NIV

Saul thought he had won a great victory over the Amalekites. God, however, saw it as a great failure because Saul had disobeyed him and then lied to Samuel about the results of the battle. Saul may have thought his lie wouldn't be detected or that what he did was not wrong. But he was mistaken.

Dishonest people soon begin to believe the lies they construct around themselves. Then they lose the ability to tell the difference between telling the truth and lying. By believing your own lies, you will move away from God. That is why honesty is so important in our relationships, both with God and with others.

God Hates Lying

Bible Reading: 1 Samuel 21:1-7; 22:9-19

Key Verse: *So David said to Ahimelech the priest, "The king has ordered me on some business, and said to me, 'Do not let*

anyone know anything about the business on which I send you, or what I have commanded you.'"

1 Samuel 21:2, NKJV

David lied to protect himself from Saul (21:10). Some excuse this lie because a war was going on and it is the duty of a good soldier to deceive the enemy. But nowhere is David's lie condoned. Even though David's small lie seemed harmless enough, it led to the death of eighty-five priests. The Bible makes it very clear that lying is wrong (Leviticus 19:11). Lying, like every other sin, is serious in God's sight and may lead to all sorts of harmful consequences. All sins must be avoided, regardless of whether or not we can foresee their potential consequences.

Harmless Lies?

Bible Reading: Psalm 12:1-8

Key Verses: *May the LORD cut off all flattering lips, the tongue that makes great boasts, those who say, "With our tongues we will prevail; our lips are our own—who is our master?"*

Psalm 12:3-4, NRSV

We may be tempted to believe that lies are relatively harmless, even useful at times. But deceit, flattery, boasting, and lies are not overlooked by God. Each of these sins originates from a bad attitude that is eventually expressed in our speech. The tongue can be our greatest enemy because, though small, it can do great damage (James 3:5). Be careful how you use yours.

CHECK IT OUT:

Genesis 12:11-13. *Lying only makes problems worse.*
Exodus 20:16. *God commands us not to lie.*
Proverbs 6:12-19. *God hates it when we lie.*
Matthew 11:16-19. *Lying can become a habit.*
Matthew 15:18-20. *Lying comes from your heart.*
Acts 5:1-11. *Lying's consequences can be deadly.*
Ephesians 4:25. *Lying hurts everyone.*
1 John 1:10. *We lie if we say we haven't ever sinned.*

MARRIAGE

Oneness

Bible Reading: Genesis 2:18-24

Key Verse: *Therefore a man shall leave his father and mother and be joined to his wife, and they shall become one flesh.*
Genesis 2:24, NKJV

God's creative work was not complete until he made woman. He could have made her from the dust of the ground, as he made man. Instead, God chose to make her from the man's flesh and bone. In so doing, he illustrated that in marriage man and woman symbolically become one flesh. This is a mystical union of the couple's hearts and lives. Throughout the Bible, God treats this special partnership seriously. One of the key principles for a successful marriage is commitment.

Marriage is based on commitment, not emotions. The emotional rush two people feel when they fall in love is wonderful, but it's a terribly inadequate basis for marriage. While physical attraction, romance, and passion are tremendous, God-given elements of a love relationship, they cannot make for lifetime commitment. To survive the pressure and temptations that attack every marriage, both husband and wife have to be totally committed to making it work. When the romance isn't quite so overwhelming and the stresses pile up, the husband and wife must stand strong in their commitment.

When seen from God's perspective, marriage can be one of God's greatest gifts. Whether or not you marry—and what happens if you do marry—is up to you. If you are planning to be married, are you willing to keep the commitment that makes the two of you one? The goal in marriage must be more than physical passion or even friendship—it should be oneness. Marriage is holy ground—no one should enter it lightly.

No Compromise

Bible Reading: 1 Kings 11:1-13

Key Verse: *As Solomon grew old, his wives turned his heart after other gods, and his heart was not fully devoted to the* LORD *his God, as the heart of David his father had been.*

1 Kings 11:4, NIV

Solomon handled great pressures in running the government, but he could not handle the pressures from his wives who wanted him to worship their gods. In marriage and other close friendships, it is difficult to resist pressure to compromise. Our love leads us to identify with the desires of those we care about.

Faced with such pressure, Solomon at first *resisted* it, maintaining pure faith. Then he *tolerated* a more widespread practice of idolatry. Finally he himself became involved in idolatrous worship, *rationalizing* away the potential danger to himself and the kingdom. It is because people naturally wish to identify with those they love that God told Solomon (and us) not to marry those who do not share our commitment to him.

Being Truly United

Bible Reading: Ezra 9:1-15

Key Verse: *For they have taken some of their daughters as wives for themselves and for their sons, so that the holy race has intermingled with the peoples of the lands; indeed, the hands of the princes and the rulers have been foremost in this unfaithfulness.*   Ezra 9:2, NASB

Some Israelites had married heathen spouses and lost track of God's purpose for them. The New Testament says that believers should not marry unbelievers (2 Corinthians 6:14). Such marriages cannot have unity on the most important issue in life—commitment and obedience to God. Because marriage involves two people becoming one, faith becomes an issue. One spouse may have to compromise beliefs for the sake of unity. Don't allow emotion or passion to blind you to the ultimate importance of marrying someone with whom you can truly be united.

"Till Death Do Us Part"

Bible Reading: Mark 10:2-12

Key Verses: *But from the beginning of the creation, God "made them male and female. For this reason a man shall leave his father and mother and be joined to his wife, and the two shall become one flesh"; so then they are no longer two, but one flesh.*　　　　　　　　　Mark 10:6-8, NKJV

Some religious leaders of Jesus' day permitted a man to divorce his wife for nearly any reason. That's why Jesus' words about divorce shocked his listeners (see Matthew 19:10) just as they shake today's readers. Jesus said in unmistakable terms that marriage is a lifetime commitment. To leave your spouse for another person may be legal, but it is adultery in God's eyes. As you think about marriage, remember that God intends it to be a permanent commitment.

What about Commitment?

Bible Reading: 1 Corinthians 7:1-40

Key Verse: *So then, he who marries his fiancée does well; and he who refrains from marriage will do better.*
　　　　　　　　　1 Corinthians 7:38, NRSV

Many people think that finding the right boyfriend or girlfriend, and especially getting married, will solve all their problems. It does feel good to have someone special, someone who cares for you and whom you care for. But no relationship, even marriage, is a "cure for whatever ails you"! For example, here are a few of the problems even marriage won't solve: (1) loneliness, (2) sexual temptation, (3) satisfaction of one's deepest emotional needs, (4) elimination of life's difficulties. Marriage alone does not hold two people together, but commitment does—commitment to Christ and to each other despite conflicts and problems. Marriage can be great, but it isn't the solution to your problems. There is only one reliable solution for everyone: Trust in Christ! He, not humans, can solve your problems.

What It Means to "Submit"

Bible Reading: 1 Corinthians 11:1-12

Key Verse: *But I want you to understand that Christ is the head of every man, and the man is the head of a woman, and God is the head of Christ.* 1 Corinthians 11:3, NASB

Submission is a key element in the smooth functioning of any business, government, or family. God ordained submission in certain relationships to prevent chaos. We must understand, however, that submission is not surrender, withdrawal, or apathy. And it does not mean inferiority—God created all people in his image, and all have equal value. Rather, submission is mutual commitment and cooperation.

Thus God calls for submission among *equals.* He did not make the man superior—he made a way for the man and woman to work together. Jesus Christ, although equal with God the Father, submitted to him to carry out the plan for salvation. Likewise, although equal to man under God, the wife should submit to her husband for the sake of their marriage and family. Submission between equals is submission by choice, not force.

CHECK IT OUT:

Genesis 2:18-24. *Marriage is God's idea.*

Genesis 24:58-60. *Commitment is essential to a successful marriage.*

Genesis 26:8. *Romance is important.*

Deuteronomy 24:5. *Newlyweds need a strong start.*

Proverbs 6:32-35. *Adultery is sinful and destructive.*

Jeremiah 7:34. *Marriage holds times of great joy.*

Hosea 1:2. *Marriage is an illustration of our relationship with God.*

Malachi 2:13-17. *God hates divorce.*

Matthew 19:3-6; Luke 16:18. *Marriage is forever.*

John 2:1-11. *Jesus' first miracle saved a wedding reception.*

Ephesians 5:21-33. *Paul reveals God's structure for marriage.*

Hebrews 13:4. *Honor your marriage vows.*

(see also Divorce)

MONEY

Giving, Sharing

Bible Reading: Numbers 31:25-54

Key Verse: *From the Israelites' half, select one out of every fifty, whether persons, cattle, donkeys, sheep, goats or other animals. Give them to the Levites, who are responsible for the care of the LORD's tabernacle.* Numbers 31:30, NIV

Moses told the Israelites to give a portion of the war spoils to God. Another portion was to go to the people who remained behind. Similarly, the money we earn is not ours alone. Everything we possess comes directly or indirectly from God and ultimately belongs to him. We should return a portion to him and also share a portion with those in need.

Wrong Motives

Bible Reading: 2 Kings 5:14-27

Key Verse: *Gehazi, the servant of Elisha the man of God, thought, "My master has let that Aramean Naaman off too lightly by not accepting from him what he offered. As the LORD lives, I will run after him and get something out of him."*
2 Kings 5:20, NRSV

Gehazi saw a perfect opportunity to get rich by self-ishly asking for the reward Elisha had refused. Unfortunately, there were three problems with his plan: (1) He willingly accepted money for what he didn't do; (2) he wrongly implied that money could be exchanged for God's free gift of healing and mercy; and (3) he lied and tried to cover up his motives for accepting the money. Although Gehazi had been a helpful servant, personal gain had become more important to him than serving God.

This passage is not teaching that money is evil. Instead, it is warning against obtaining it wrongly. It also teaches that true service is motivated by love and devotion to God and seeks no personal gain. As you serve God, check your motives—you can't serve both God and money (Matthew 6:24).

True Treasure

Bible Reading: Psalm 37:1-17

Key Verse: *Do not fret because of evil men or be envious of those who do wrong.* Psalm 37:1, NIV

We should never envy the wicked, even though some of them may be extremely popular or excessively rich. No matter how much they have, it will fade and vanish like grass that withers and dies. Those who follow God live in a different manner than the wicked and, in the end, have far greater treasures in heaven. What the unbeliever gets lasts a lifetime, if he or she is lucky. What you get from following God lasts forever.

Selfish Spending

Bible Reading: Hosea 10:1-7

Key Verse: *Israel was a spreading vine; he brought forth fruit for himself. As his fruit increased, he built more altars; as his land prospered, he adorned his sacred stones.* Hosea 10:1, NIV

Israel prospered under Jeroboam II, gaining military and economic strength. But the more prosperous Israel became, the more it spent on her idols. It seems as if the more God gives, the more we spend. We want bigger houses, better cars, finer clothes, and more expensive education. But the finest things the world offers line the pathway to destruction. As you prosper, consider where your money is going. Is it being used for God's purposes, or are you spending it all on yourself?

Giving Back to God

Bible Reading: Malachi 3:6-18

Key Verse: *"Bring the whole tithe into the storehouse, that there may be food in my house. Test me in this," says the* LORD *Almighty, "and see if I will not throw open the floodgates of heaven and pour out so much blessing that you will not have room enough for it."* Malachi 3:10, NIV

In these verses, God warned his people that refusing to give him tithes and offerings (that is, returning a portion of what he had given them) was actually stealing from him! God knows how powerful money is. Jesus talked about money more than he talked about anything else. That's because money, unlike any other possession, can take a strong foothold in our life. It can even control us. Money itself is not evil. It's when we love it, make it our only purpose in life, and believe that it can solve all our troubles that money becomes evil for us. When money becomes our god, we're in big trouble.

You may not have a lot of money, and what little you have probably gets spent on yourself. Maybe you think you couldn't spare a dime for somebody else. Maybe you think that because you have so little, God doesn't need you to give. Actually, God *doesn't need* your money. He owns everything already! But *we* need to give it away because we need to control our money, not let it control us.

So how do we keep the love of money from overpowering us? The best way is to learn the joy of giving it away. And you can begin to build that habit while you're young. Here is a way to start giving your money back to God. Each time you get some, take 10 percent out and put it aside for God. Do this for a month, and don't worry about how much or how little the amount is.

Next, decide where or to whom you want to give your money. Maybe you could give it to a missionary. Maybe you'll want to give it to your church. Maybe you'll do both. Remember, the amount doesn't matter; what matters is your attitude and giving what you can. In so doing, you are furthering God's kingdom and making a wise investment for eternity. When you stay in control of your money by willingly giving what you can, then you can be sure money will never control you.

Don't Let It Separate You from God

Bible Reading: Mark 10:17-27

Key Verse: *Jesus, looking at him, loved him and said, "You lack one thing; go, sell what you own, and give the money to the poor, and you will have treasure in heaven; then come, follow me."* Mark 10:21, NRSV

This young man wanted to be sure he would have eternal life. Although he said he'd never once broken any of the laws Jesus mentioned, and perhaps he had kept the Pharisees' loophole-filled version of them, he asked Jesus what he could *do*. Jesus' response lovingly challenged the young man's true love: "Sell all you have and give to the poor." Here was the barrier that could keep this young man out of the kingdom: his love of money. Money represented his pride of accomplishment and self-effort. Ironically, the young man's attitude made him unable to keep the first commandment, to let nothing be more important than God (Exodus 20:3). He could not meet the one requirement Jesus gave—to turn his whole heart and life over to God. The man came to Jesus wondering what he could do—he left seeing what he was unable to do. What barriers are keeping you from turning your life over to Christ?

Do You Love Money?

Bible Reading: 1 Timothy 6:6-19

Key Verse: *For the love of money is a root of all kinds of evil, and in their eagerness to be rich some have wandered away from the faith and pierced themselves with many pains.* 1 Timothy 6:10, NRSV

Despite overwhelming evidence to the contrary, some people still believe money brings happiness. Rich people craving greater riches can be caught in an endless cycle that only ends in ruin and desperation. How can you avoid the love of money? Paul gives us five principles to live by: (1) Realize that one day riches will all be gone (6:7, 17); (2) be content with what you have (6:8); (3) watch what you are willing to do to get more money (6:9-10); (4) love people and God's work more than money (6:11, 18); and (5) freely share what you have with others (6:18).

Spiritually Bankrupt

Bible Reading: Hebrews 13:5-7

Key Verse: *Keep your lives free from the love of money and be content with what you have, because God has said, "Never will I leave you; never will I forsake you."*

Hebrews 13:5, NIV

Government leaders, businesses, families, even churches get trapped into thinking money is the answer to every problem. As a result, people spend money on their problems. But just as the thrill of liquor is only temporary, the soothing effect of the last dollar spent soon wears off and people have to spend more. Scripture recognizes that money is necessary for survival, but it warns against the love of money (see Matthew 6:24; 1 Timothy 6:10). Money is dangerous because it deceives us into thinking that wealth is the easiest way to get everything we want. The love of money is sinful because we trust *it*, rather than God, to solve our problems. Those who pursue money's empty promises will one day discover that they have nothing, because they are spiritually bankrupt.

CHECK IT OUT:

Psalm 119:33-42. *Money should not be life's goal.*
Proverbs 15:27. *Money gotten dishonestly causes pain.*
Ecclesiastes 5:10-11; Luke 12:15. *Money never satisfies.*
Matthew 6:19-21. *Never put your money above God.*
Mark 12:41-44. *Gladly give what you can.*
Luke 16:13. *Do you own your money, or does it own you?*
1 Timothy 6:5. *Stay away from money-hungry preachers.*
1 Timothy 6:17-19. *Having money carries responsibility.*
James 5:1-6. *Money is gone when we die.*

OBEDIENCE

What Does God Want?

Bible Reading: Genesis 4:1-7; John 14:15-21

Key Verse: *They who have my commandments and keep them are those who love me; and those who love me will be loved by my Father, and I will love them and reveal myself to them.* John 14:21, NRSV

What does God expect of us? How can we please him? The two passages listed above give us the two keys to pleasing God. The first key is found in the story of Cain and Abel. Both of these men brought something to God, but only Abel's sacrifice pleased God. One reason was because Cain's heart was not really in it. He tried to please God out of obligation instead of love. So the first key to pleasing God is found in our heart or our *motivation*. Do we really want to make God happy, or are we going through the motions because someone told us we should?

The second key is found in Jesus' words to his disciples. If we love him, we *obey* him. Obediencc to God is loving him enough to listen to what he says, then following through on what we know he is telling us. That's why it's so important to read the Bible every day.

Obedience is not about giving things up. It's about replacing some old actions and attitudes with better ones, living your life with a definite goal and purpose—to spend eternity with God.

Why We Obey God

Bible Reading: Genesis 17:1-8

Key Verse: *When Abram was ninety-nine years old, the LORD appeared to him and said, "I am God Almighty; walk before me and be blameless."* Genesis 17:1, NIV

The Lord told Abram, "I am God; therefore obey me and live as you should." God has the same message for us today. We are to obey him because he is God—that is reason enough. If you don't think the benefits are worth it, consider who God is—the only one with the power and ability to meet your every need.

Obey God's Commands

Bible Reading: Leviticus 10:1-7

Key Verse: *And fire came out from the presence of the LORD and consumed them, and they died before the LORD.*

Leviticus 10:2, NASB

Aaron's sons were careless about following the laws for sacrifices. In response, God destroyed them with a blast of fire. Performing the sacrifices was an act of obedience. Doing them correctly showed respect for God. It is easy for us to grow careless about obeying God, to live our way instead of his. But if one way were just as good as another, God would not command us to live his way. He always has good reasons for his commands, and we always place ourselves in danger when we consciously or carelessly disobey them.

Determine to Obey

Bible Reading: 1 Samuel 26:1-25

Key Verse: *"Now behold, as your life was highly valued in my sight this day, so may my life be highly valued in the sight of the LORD, and may He deliver me from all distress."*

1 Samuel 26:24, NASB

The strongest moral decisions are the ones we make before temptation strikes. David was determined to follow God, and this carried over into his decision not to murder God's chosen king, Saul, even when his men and the circumstances seemed to make it a feasible option. Who would you have been like in such a situation—David or David's men? To be like David and follow God, we must realize that we can't do wrong in order to execute justice. Even when our closest friends counsel us to do something that seems right, we must always put God's commands first.

Take God's Commands Seriously

Bible Reading: 1 Kings 11:1-13

Key Verse: *They were from nations about which the LORD had told the Israelites, "You must not intermarry with them, because they will surely turn your hearts after their gods." Nevertheless, Solomon held fast to them in love.*
1 Kings 11:2, NIV

Although Solomon had clear instructions from God *not* to marry women from foreign nations, he chose to disregard God's commands. He married not one but many heathen wives, who subsequently led him away from God. God knows our human strengths and weaknesses, and his commands are always for our good. Some people ignore God's commands, but there are inevitable negative consequences resulting from such action. It is not enough to know God's Word or even to believe it—we must follow it and apply it to life's daily activities and decisions. Take God's commands seriously. Like Solomon, the "wisest man who ever lived," we are not as strong as we may think.

Lip Service

Bible Reading: 2 Kings 10:30-36

Key Verse: *But Jehu took no heed to walk in the law of the LORD God of Israel with all his heart; for he did not depart from the sins of Jeroboam, who had made Israel sin.* 2 Kings 10:31, NKJV

Jehu did much of what the Lord told him to, but he did not obey him with all his heart. He had become God's *instrument* for carrying out justice, but he had not become God's *servant*. As a result, he gave only lip service to God while he worshiped the golden calves. Like Jehu, we can be very active in our work for God and still not give the heartfelt obedience he desires. Check your heart attitude toward God. If you're just giving him lip service, it's time to make a change.

Active and Passive Obedience

Bible Reading: 1 Chronicles 10:1-14

Key Verses: *Saul died because he was unfaithful to the LORD; he did not keep the word of the LORD and even consulted a medium for guidance, and did not inquire of the LORD.*
1 Chronicles 10:13-14, NIV

Saul's disobedience was both active and passive—he not only did wrong, but he also *failed* to do right. He actively disobeyed by attempting murder, ignoring God's instructions, and seeking guidance from a medium. He passively disobeyed by neglecting to ask God for guidance as he ran the kingdom. Obedience, too, is both passive and active. It is not enough just to avoid what is wrong; we need to actively pursue what is right.

Obedience First

Bible Reading: 1 Chronicles 15:1-15

Key Verses: *He said to them, "You are the heads of families of the Levites; sanctify yourselves, you and your kindred, so that you may bring up the ark of the LORD, the God of Israel, to the place that I have prepared for it. Because you did not carry it the first time, the LORD our God burst out against us, because we did not give it proper care."*
1 Chronicles 15:12-13, NRSV

When David's first attempt to move the ark failed (1 Chronicles 13:8-14), he learned an important lesson: When God gives specific instructions, it is wise to follow them precisely. This time David saw to it that the Levites carried the ark (Numbers 4:5-15). We may not fully understand the reasons behind God's instructions, but we can know that his wisdom is complete and his judgment infallible. The way to know God's instructions is to know his Word. But just as children do not understand the reasons for all their parents' instructions until they are adults, we will not understand all of God's instructions in this life. It is far better to obey God first, and then seek to know the reasons later.

Willing to Stand Alone

Bible Reading: Jeremiah 38:1-13

Key Verse: *My lord the king, these men have acted wickedly in all that they have done to Jeremiah the prophet whom they have cast into the cistern.* Jeremiah 38:9, NASB

Ebed-melech feared God more than man. He alone among the palace officials stood up against the murder plot. His obedience could have cost him his life. Because he obeyed, however, he was spared when Jerusalem fell (39:15-18). You can either go along with the crowd or speak up for God. When someone is treated unkindly or unjustly, reach out to that person with God's love. You may be the only one who does. When you're being treated unkindly yourself, be sure to thank God when he sends an "Ebed-melech" your way.

Tough Obedience

Bible Reading: Hosea 1:1-3

Key Verse: *When the LORD began to speak through Hosea, the LORD said to him, "Go, take to yourself an adulterous wife and children of unfaithfulness, because the land is guilty of the vilest adultery in departing from the LORD."* Hosea 1:2, NIV

It is hard to imagine Hosea's feelings when God told him to marry a woman who would be unfaithful to him. He may not have wanted to do this. But he obeyed. God often asked his prophets who were facing extraordinary times to be extraordinarily obedient. He may ask you to do something difficult and extraordinary, too. If he does, how will you respond? Will you obey him, trusting that he who knows everything has a special purpose for his request? Will you be satisfied with the knowledge that the pain involved in obedience may benefit those you serve, and not you personally?

Actions and Words

Bible Reading: Matthew 21:28-32

Key Verse: *Then the father went to the other son and said the same thing. He answered, "I will, sir," but he did not go.*
Matthew 21:30, NIV

The son who said he would obey and then didn't represented the nation of Israel in Jesus' day. They said they wanted to do God's will, but they constantly disobeyed. It is dangerous to pretend to obey God when our hearts are far from him, because God knows our intentions. Our actions must match our words.

CHECK IT OUT:

Genesis 6:22. *Noah obeyed God.*

Genesis 22:1-12. *Put God first in your life.*

Exodus 8:25-29. *Never compromise your obedience to God.*

1 Kings 17:13-16. *Obedience can lead to a miracle.*

Proverbs 6:20-23. *Obey your parents.*

Matthew 1:18-25. *Obey God; don't please people.*

Matthew 2:13-15, 19-23. *Obeying God can save your life.*

Matthew 4:18-22. *Obey Christ when he calls.*

Luke 1:38. *Obey, no matter what the cost.*

Hebrews 11:7. *Others may scoff at your obedience.*

(see also Bible and God's Will)

OCCULT

Telling the Future

Bible Reading: Leviticus 20:6-9, 27

Key Verse: *If any turn to mediums and wizards, prostituting themselves to them, I will set my face against them, and will cut them off from the people.* Leviticus 20:6, NRSV

Everyone is interested in what the future holds, and we often look to others for guidance. But God warned his people about getting advice from occult sources. Therefore, mediums and wizards were outlawed because God was not the source of their information. At best, occult practitioners are fakes whose predictions cannot be trusted. At worst, they are in contact with evil spirits and are thus extremely dangerous. We don't need to look to the occult for information about the future. God has given us the Bible so that we may

obtain all the information we need—and the Bible's
teaching is trustworthy.

Evil Sources

Bible Reading: Deuteronomy 18:9-14

Key Verse: *For whoever does these things is detestable to the LORD; and
because of these detestable things the LORD your God will
drive them out before you.*   Deuteronomy 18:12, NASB

Just as most of us are naturally curious about a magi-
cian's tricks, the Israelites were curious about the
occult practices of the Canaanite religions. But Satan
is behind the occult, and God flatly forbade Israel to
have anything to do with it. Today, people are still fas-
cinated by horoscopes, fortune-telling, witchcraft,
and bizarre cults. Often their interest comes from a
desire to know and control the future. But Satan is no
less dangerous today than he was in Moses' time. In
the Bible, God tells us all we need to know about what
is going to happen. The information Satan offers is
likely to be distorted or completely false. With the
trustworthy guidance of the Holy Spirit through the
Scriptures and the church, we don't need to turn to
occult sources for faulty information.

God's Power Alone

Bible Reading: Acts 19:13-20

Key Verse: *Some Jews who went around driving out evil spirits tried
to invoke the name of the Lord Jesus over those who were
demon-possessed.*   Acts 19:13, NIV

Ephesus was considered a center for black magic and
other occult practices. The people sought spells to give
them wealth, happiness, and success in marriage.
Superstition and sorcery were commonplace. Many
Ephesians engaged in exorcism and occult practices for
profit, even sending demons from people. The sons of
Sceva were impressed by Paul's work, whose power to
cast out demons came from God's Holy Spirit, not from
witchcraft, and was obviously more powerful than

theirs. They discovered, however, that no person can control or duplicate God's power. These men were calling upon the name without knowing the person. It is knowing Jesus, not reciting his name like a magic charm, that gives us the power to change people. Christ works his power only through those he chooses, which does not include people who dabble in the occult. If you are mixed up in the occult, learn a lesson from the Ephesians, and get rid of anything that lures you into such practices.

CHECK IT OUT:

Deuteronomy 4:19; 17:2-5. *Don't get involved with astrology or horoscopes, even for fun.*
1 Samuel 28:3-8. *Saul consults a medium.*
2 Chronicles 33:6. *Manasseh was an evil example.*
Isaiah 47:12-15. *Astrology is useless.*
Jeremiah 10:2. *Horoscopes are worthless.*
Matthew 7:15. *Cults are from Satan.*
2 Timothy 3:6-7. *Compare new ideas with God's Word.*

(see also Future)

PARENTS
(SEE AUTHORITY)

PARTYING

Harmless Recreation?

Bible Reading: Numbers 25:1-9

Key Verse: *While Israel was staying at Shittim, the people began to have sexual relations with the women of Moab.*

Numbers 25:1, NRSV

Attending a local party with the Moabite girls may have seemed harmless enough. But for these young Israelite men, "fun" turned into tragedy. At first, they didn't think about worshiping idols. They just wanted to go to the party and have a good time. Before long, they started attending local feasts and family celebrations that involved idol worship. Soon they were in over their heads, absorbed into the practices of the heathen culture. Their desire for fun and companionship caused them to loosen their spiritual commitment. What about your favorite recreations—do they help you grow in faith, or do they push you to relax your standards?

CHECK IT OUT:

1 Corinthians 9:25. *Do parties help you be your best?*

1 Corinthians 10:31. *Glorify God in all you do.*

1 Corinthians 10:32. *Your actions could make others stumble.*

1 Peter 4:1-6. *Stay away from wild parties.*

(see also Drinking and Drugs)

PATIENCE

Are You Willing to Wait?

Bible Reading: Genesis 29:15-30

Key Verse: *And Jacob did so. He finished the week with Leah, and then Laban gave him his daughter Rachel to be his wife.*

Genesis 29:28, NIV

People often wonder if waiting a long time for something they want is worth it. Jacob waited seven years to marry Rachel. After being tricked, he agreed to work seven more years for her! The most important goals and desires are worth working and waiting for. Movies and television have created the illusion that people have to wait only about an hour to solve their problems or get what they want. Don't be trapped into thinking the same is true in real life. Patience is hardest when we need it the most, but it is the key to achieving our goals.

Time of Preparation

Bible Reading: 2 Samuel 5:1-5

Key Verse: *So all the elders of Israel came to the king at Hebron, and King David made a covenant with them before the LORD at Hebron; then they anointed David king over Israel.*

2 Samuel 5:3, NASB

David did not become king of all Israel until he was thirty-seven years old, although he had been promised the kingship many years earlier (1 Samuel 16:13). During those years, David had to wait patiently for the fulfillment of God's promise. If you feel pressured to achieve instant results and success, remember David's patience. Just as his time of waiting prepared him for his important task, a waiting period may help prepare you by strengthening your spiritual character.

God's Perfect Timing

Bible Reading: Psalm 75:1-10

Key Verse: *When I choose the proper time, I will judge uprightly.*

Psalm 75:2, NKJV

Children have difficulty grasping the concept of time. "It's not time yet" is not a reason they easily understand. They only comprehend the present. As limited human beings, we can't comprehend God's perspective on time. We want everything now, not recognizing that God's timing is better for us. When God is ready, he will do what needs to be done. We may be impatient as children, but it is clear that God's timing is perfect, and we should accept it.

When Evil Runs Rampant

Bible Reading: Habakkuk 2:1-6

Key Verse: *For the vision is yet for the appointed time; it hastens toward the goal, and it will not fail. Though it tarries, wait for it; for it will certainly come, it will not delay.*
Habakkuk 2:3, NASB

Evil seems to have the upper hand in the world. Habakkuk complained vigorously to God about it. God's answer to him was "Be patient! I will work out my plans." Like Habakkuk, Christians often feel angry and discouraged by the evil they see going on in the world. Being patient isn't easy, but it helps to remember that God hates sin even more than we do. Therefore, punishment of sin will certainly come. In the meantime, trust God even when you don't understand why evil events occur as they do.

A Chance to Grow

Bible Reading: Romans 5:1-5

Key Verses: *Not only so, but we also rejoice in our sufferings, because we know that suffering produces perseverance; perseverance, character; and character, hope.*
Romans 5:3-4, NIV

Paul tells us that in the future we will *become*, but until then we must *overcome*. This means we will experience difficulties that help us grow. Problems we run into will develop our patience—which in turn will strengthen our character, deepen our trust in God, and give us greater confidence about the future. You probably find your patience tested in some way every day. Thank God for these opportunities to grow, and deal with them in his strength (see also James 1:2-4; 1 Peter 1:6-7).

Waiting for Justice

Bible Reading: Revelation 6:9-11

Key Verse: *Then a white robe was given to each of them; and it was said to them that they should rest a little while longer, until both the number of their fellow servants and their brethren, who would be killed as they were, was completed.* Revelation 6:11, NKJV

The martyrs are eager for God to bring justice to the earth, but they are told to wait. Those who suffer and die for their faith will not be forgotten, nor do they die in vain. Rather, they will be singled out by God for special honor. We may wish for justice immediately, as these martyrs did, but we must be patient. God works on his own timetable, and he promises justice. No suffering for the sake of God's kingdom, however, is wasted effort.

CHECK IT OUT:

> 1 Samuel 13:8-14. *Lack of patience can cause you to miss blessings.*
> Luke 15:11-24. *God is our patient Father.*
> Romans 8:24-30. *Patiently look for the positive in life.*
> 1 Corinthians 13:4. *Love is patient.*
> Galatians 5:22. *Patience is a fruit of the Spirit.*
> Ephesians 4:2. *Be patient with other believers.*
> 2 Thessalonians 1:4-5. *Patience helps you to endure suffering.*
> Hebrews 11:13-16. *Focus on heaven for patience.*
> James 1:2-4. *Troubles teach patience.*

PEACE

Only God Gives True Peace and Security

Bible Reading: 1 Chronicles 29:10-20

Key Verse: *Yours, O LORD, are the greatness, the power, the glory, the*

victory, and the majesty; for all that is in the heavens
and on the earth is yours; yours is the kingdom, O LORD,
and you are exalted as head above all.

1 Chronicles 29:11, NRSV

David knew God and acknowledged his greatness and
control over everything. Our constantly changing world
is controlled by a constant and unchanging God. As we
see life come and go, objects fade, materials decay, and
friends change, the only thing on which we can truly
depend is God's control. His love and purpose for us
never change. Only when we understand this can we
have real peace and security.

CHECK IT OUT:

> 2 Chronicles 14:7. *Peace is not necessarily a time of rest.*
> Psalm 3:5. *Peace comes from the assurance of answered*
> *prayer.*
> Matthew 5:25-26. *Make peace with others quickly.*
> Colossians 3:14-15. *Peace can affect our decisions.*
> 1 Peter 3:11. *Peace must be active, not passive.*

PEER PRESSURE

Keep Yourself Pure

Bible Reading: Leviticus 18:1-5, 24-30

Key Verse: *Do not defile yourselves in any of these ways, for by all*
these practices the nations I am casting out before you
have defiled themselves. Leviticus 18:24, NRSV

The Israelites moved from one idol-infested country to
another. As God helped them form a new culture, he
warned them to leave all aspects of their heathen back-
ground behind. He also warned them how easy it would
be to slip into the heathen culture of Canaan, where the
society and religions appealed to carnal desires, especially sexual immorality and drunkenness. God did not
want his people absorbed into the surrounding culture
and environment. Therefore the Israelites were to keep
themselves pure and set apart for God.

Society may pressure us to conform to its way of life and thought, but yielding to that pressure will (1) create confusion as to which side we should be on, and (2) eliminate our effectiveness in serving God. Follow God, and don't let the culture around you mold your thoughts and actions.

Pressured to Disobey

Bible Reading: Judges 2:1-14

Key Verse: *They forsook the LORD, the God of their fathers, who had brought them out of Egypt. They followed and worshiped various gods of the peoples around them. They provoked the LORD to anger* — Judges 2:12, NIV

This generation of Israelites abandoned the faith of their parents and began worshiping the gods of their neighbors. Many things can tempt us to abandon what we know is right. The desire to be accepted by others can lead us into behavior that is unacceptable to God. Don't be pressured into disobedience.

Copycats

Bible Reading: 2 Kings 17:7-23

Key Verse: *This occurred because the people of Israel had sinned against the LORD their God, who had brought them up out of the land of Egypt from under the hand of Pharaoh king of Egypt. They had worshiped other gods.* — 2 Kings 17:7, NRSV

The Lord judged the people of Israel because they copied the evil customs of the surrounding nations, worshiping false gods, accommodating pagan customs, and following their own desires. It is not safe to copy the world's customs, because godless people tend to live selfishly. To live for yourself, as Israel learned, brings serious consequences from God.

Sometimes it is difficult and painful to follow God, but consider the alternative. You can live for God, or you can eternally die for yourself. Determine to be God's person and do what he says, regardless of the cost. What God thinks of you is infinitely more important than what the world thinks. (See Romans 12:1-2 and 1 John 2:15-17.)

Too Embarrassed

Bible Reading: Matthew 14:1-12

Key Verse: *And although he was grieved, the king commanded it to be given because of his oaths, and because of his dinner guests.*   Matthew 14:9, NASB

Herod did not want to kill John the Baptist, but he gave the order so he wouldn't be embarrassed in front of his guests. How easy it is to give in to crowd pressure and to let ourselves be coerced into doing wrong. Do your best to stay out of situations where it is too embarrassing to do what is right. But if you get in a situation like this, do what is right, no matter how embarrassing or painful it may be.

Salt in a Stale World

Bible Reading: Luke 14:25-35

Key Verse: *Salt is good; but if salt has lost its taste, how can its saltiness be restored?*   Luke 14:34, NRSV

Salt can lose its flavor. When it gets wet and then dries, nothing is left but a tasteless residue. Many Christians avoid the cost of standing for Christ by blending into the world. But Jesus says if Christians lose their distinctive "saltiness," they become worthless. Just as salt flavors and preserves food, we are to preserve the good in the world, help keep it from spoiling, and bring new flavor to life. This requires planning, willing sacrifice, and unswerving commitment to Christ and his kingdom. Being "salty" is not easy, but if a Christian fails in this function, he or she fails to represent Christ in the world. How "salty" are you?

CHECK IT OUT:

Genesis 39:1-9. *Don't let others pressure you into sin.*
Psalm 1:1-2. *Don't conform to the wrong crowd.*
Exodus 32:1-10. *Never conform to those who stand against God.*

Nehemiah 4. *Nehemiah demonstrated how to stand against pressure.*

Proverbs 1:10-19. *Giving in to peer pressure isn't worth the risks.*

Daniel 6:1-22. *Daniel refused to conform.*

Romans 12:1-2. *Don't copy the world.*

Colossians 2:23. *Develop faith, not just appearance.*

1 John 2:15-17. *Turn away from this evil world and all it offers.*

PERSISTENCE

Persistence Pays Off

Bible Reading: Genesis 31:38-44

Key Verse: *Unless the God of my father, the God of Abraham and the Fear of Isaac, had been with me, surely now you would have sent me away empty-handed. God has seen my affliction and the labor of my hands, and rebuked you last night.* Genesis 31:42, NKJV

Jacob made it a habit to do more than was expected of him. When his flocks were attacked, he took the losses rather than splitting them with Laban. He worked hard even after several pay cuts. His diligence eventually paid off—his flocks began to multiply. Making a habit of doing more than expected can pay off. It (1) pleases God, (2) earns recognition and advancement, (3) enhances your reputation, (4) builds others' confidence in you, (5) gives you more experience and knowledge, and (6) develops your spiritual maturity.

For the Right Cause

Bible Reading: 2 Samuel 2:17-28

Key Verse: *Then Abner said to him, "Turn aside to the right or to the left; take on one of the young men and strip him of his weapons." But Asahel would not stop chasing him.* 2 Samuel 2:21, NIV

Abner repeatedly warned Asahel to turn back or risk losing his life, but Asahel refused to turn from his self-imposed duty. Persistence is a good trait if it is for a worthy cause. But if the goal is only personal honor or gain, persistence may be no more than stubbornness. Asahel's stubbornness not only cost him his life but also spurred unfortunate disunity in David's army for years to come (3:26-27; 1 Kings 2:28-35). Before you decide to pursue a goal, make sure it is worthy of your devotion.

Persistent in Witnessing

Bible Reading: Ezekiel 2:1-10

Key Verse: *But you shall speak My words to them whether they listen or not, for they are rebellious.*   Ezekiel 2:7, NASB

Ezekiel was given the difficult responsibility of presenting God's message to the ungrateful and abusive. Sometimes we are also called to be an example or share our faith with people who may be unkind to us. Just as the Lord told Ezekiel not to give up, he tells us to not give up and join the rebels. Rather, tell the Good News whether it is convenient or not (2 Timothy 4:2).

CHECK IT OUT:

Exodus 32:1-14. *Your persistence could save many lives.*
Matthew 13:21. *Never stop believing what Christ can do.*
Luke 11:8-10. *Persistence in prayer gets answers.*
1 Corinthians 9:24-27. *It takes persistence to live for God.*
Galatians 6:7-10. *Be persistent in doing right.*
Philippians 3:12-14. *Keep working toward your potential.*
Colossians 4:2. *Be persistent in prayer.*

POPULARITY

Warnings

Bible Reading: Leviticus 26:1-13

Key Verse: *You shall not make idols for yourselves; neither a carved image nor a sacred pillar shall you rear up for yourselves; nor shall you set up an engraved stone in your land, to bow down to it; for I am the LORD your God.*
Leviticus 26:1, NKJV

The people of the Old Testament were warned over and over against worshiping idols. We wonder how they could deceive themselves with these objects of wood and stone. Yet God could give us the same warning because we often put idols before him. Idolatry is making anything more important than God, and our lives are full of that temptation. Money, looks, success, reputation, security, popularity—these are today's idols. As you look at these false gods that promise everything you want but nothing you need, does idolatry seem so far removed from your experience?

Do-It-Yourself Fame

Bible Reading: 1 Samuel 15:17-26; 1 Chronicles 11:1-9

Key Verse: *And David became more and more powerful, because the LORD Almighty was with him.* 1 Chronicles 11:9, NIV

King Saul's power and fame decreased because he wanted all the credit for himself and ignored God. In contrast, King David's power and fame increased as a direct result of his consistent trust in God. Those who are concerned about building a name for themselves risk losing the very recognition they crave. Like David, we should be concerned more about righteousness, honesty, and excellence, and leave the fame and glory to God.

Humility

Bible Reading: 1 Samuel 18:1-30

Key Verse: *In everything he did he had great success, because the LORD was with him.* 1 Samuel 18:14, NIV

While Saul's popularity made him proud and arrogant, David remained humble even when the entire nation praised him. Although David succeeded in almost everything he tried and became famous throughout the land, he refused to use his popular support to his advantage against Saul. Don't allow popularity to twist your perception of your own importance. It's easier to

be humble when you're not on center stage, but how
will you react to praise and honor?

Pleasing People or God?

Bible Reading: 2 Samuel 3:35-36; 8:1-15

Key Verse: *So David reigned over all Israel; and David administered
justice and righteousness for all his people.*

2 Samuel 8:15, NASB

Everything David did pleased the people, not because
he tried to please them, but because he tried to please
God. Often those who try the hardest to become popular never make it. But praise from people is not that
important. Don't spend your time devising ways to
please others so you will be accepted by them. Instead,
strive to do what is right—and your convictions will be
highly respected by both God and people.

Popularity Contest

Bible Reading: Matthew 9:9-13

Key Verse: *On hearing this, Jesus said, "It is not the healthy who
need a doctor, but the sick."* Matthew 9:12, NIV

The Pharisees constantly tried to trap Jesus, and they
thought his association with these "lowlifes" was the
perfect opportunity. Their actions showed what they
valued most—the praise of people. For the Pharisees
were more concerned with criticism than encouragement, with their own appearance of holiness than in
helping people, and with outward respectability than
practical help. But God is concerned for all people,
including those who live sinful lives. The Christian life
is not a popularity contest! Following Jesus' example,
we should share the Good News with the poor, lonely,
and outcast, not just the good, talented, and popular.

CHECK IT OUT:

Matthew 3:7-10; Mark 6:27; Luke 3:19-20. *Obeying God
may make you unpopular.*

Matthew 10:32-33. *Never be so popular that you are
ashamed of Christ.*

Luke 14:25-27. *Be more popular with Christ than with people.*

John 17:14-17. *Jesus wasn't popular.*

2 Corinthians 4:4. *Satan makes his followers hate Christians.*

Colossians 1:11. *Keep on going no matter what happens.*

James 4:4. *God doesn't want us to be popular with everyone.*

1 John 2:15-17. *Believers must stay away from some popular activities.*

PRAYER

Prayer Can Change Things

Bible Reading: Exodus 32:1-14

Key Verse: *And the LORD changed his mind about the disaster that he planned to bring on his people.*   Exodus 32:14, NRSV

God was ready to destroy the whole nation because of the people's sin. But Moses pleaded for mercy, and God spared them. This is one of the countless examples in Scripture of how prayer can make a difference. Don't neglect prayer because the situation seems irreversible. Instead, make a daily prayer list, and spend time praying for others. Prayer can change things.

Follow Directions

Bible Reading: 1 Samuel 28:4-19

Key Verse: *Saul answered, "I am in great distress, for the Philistines are warring against me, and God has turned away from me and answers me no more, either by prophets or by dreams; so I have summoned you to tell me what I should do."*   1 Samuel 28:15, NRSV

God did not answer Saul's appeals because Saul had not followed God's previous directions. Sometimes people wonder why their prayers are not answered. But if they don't fulfill the responsibilities God has already given them, they should not be surprised when he does not give further guidance.

How to Pray for Yourself

Bible Reading: 1 Kings 8:54-61

Key Verse: *Let your heart therefore be wholly devoted to the LORD our God, to walk in His statutes and to keep His commandments, as at this day.*   1 Kings 8:61, NASB

Solomon blessed the people and prayed for them. His prayer can be a pattern for our prayers. He had five basic requests: (1) for God's presence (8:57); (2) for the desire to do God's will in everything (8:58); (3) for help with daily needs (8:59); (4) for the desire to live good and perfect lives (8:61); and (5) for the ability to obey God's laws and commandments (8:61). These prayer requests are just as appropriate today as in Solomon's time.

Bold Requests

Bible Reading: 2 Kings 2:9-12; Isaiah 38:1-8

Key Verse: *Go and tell Hezekiah, "This is what the LORD, the God of your father David, says: I have heard your prayer and seen your tears; I will add fifteen years to your life."*
Isaiah 38:5, NIV

In these passages, two men made two very bold requests of God. Elisha asked for twice as much power as Elijah had. This was a bold request, but God granted it. Why? Because Elisha's motives were pure. His main goal was not to be better or more powerful than Elijah, but to accomplish more for God. If our motives are pure, we don't have to be afraid to ask great things of God. Before we ask God for great power or ability, we need to examine our desires and get rid of any selfish ones we find.

Second, when Isaiah told Hezekiah of his impending death, Hezekiah immediately turned to God. God responded to his prayer, allowing him to live another fifteen years. In response to fervent prayer, God may change the course of our lives, too. Never hesitate to ask God for radical changes, providing that your motives are to honor him with the changes.

Pray First

Bible Reading: 2 Kings 19:1-19

Key Verse: *Hezekiah received the letter from the hand of the messengers and read it; then Hezekiah went up to the house of the LORD and spread it before the LORD.*

2 Kings 19:14, NRSV

Sennacherib, whose armies had captured all the fortified cities of Judah, sent a message to Hezekiah to surrender because resistance was futile. Realizing the situation was hopeless, Hezekiah's first action was to go to the temple and pray. He knew that God specializes in impossible situations. God answered Hezekiah's prayer and delivered Judah by sending an army to attack the Assyrian capital, forcing Sennacherib to leave at once. Prayer should be our first response in any crisis. Our problems are God's opportunities.

Reverent Prayer

Bible Reading: 2 Kings 19:1-19

Key Verse: *Then Hezekiah prayed before the LORD, and said: "O LORD God of Israel, the One who dwells between the cherubim, You are God, You alone, of all the kingdoms of the earth. You have made heaven and earth."*

2 Kings 19:15, NKJV

Although Hezekiah came boldly to God with his request, he did not take God for granted or approach him flippantly. Instead, he acknowledged God's sovereignty and Judah's total dependence upon him. Hezekiah's prayer provides a good model for us. We should not be afraid to approach God with our prayers, but we must come to him with respect for who he is and what he can do.

Does God Hear?

Bible Reading: Psalm 4:1-8

Key Verse: *Know that the LORD has set apart the godly for himself; the LORD will hear when I call to him.* Psalm 4:3, NIV

David knew that God heard his prayers and would answer him. We, too, can know that God listens and answers when we call on him. Sometimes we think God will not hear us because we have fallen short of his high standards for holy living. But God listens to us because we have been forgiven. When you feel that your prayers are bouncing off the ceiling, remember that as a believer you have been set apart by God and that he loves you. He hears and answers (although his answers may not be what we expect). Look at your problems in the light of God's power instead of looking at God in the light of your problems.

Tell God Everything

Bible Reading: Daniel 9:2-19

Key Verse: *So I turned to the Lord God and pleaded with him in prayer and petition, in fasting, and in sackcloth and ashes.* Daniel 9:3, NIV

Daniel knew how to pray. As he prayed, he fasted, confessed his sins, and pleaded that God would reveal his will. He prayed with complete surrender to God and with complete openness to what God was saying to him. When you pray, follow Daniel's example and talk to God with openness, vulnerability, and honesty.

Pray for Anything?

Bible Reading: Matthew 21:21-22

Key Verse: *If you believe, you will receive whatever you ask for in prayer.* Matthew 21:22, NIV

Jesus' words that we can get anything we ask in prayer are not a guarantee that Jesus will give us anything we want. God does not grant requests that would hurt us or others, or that violate his own nature or will. Jesus' statement is not a blank check—our prayers must focus on the work of God's kingdom. Then we may go to him in peace and confidence, knowing he will respond to us in his love and wisdom.

Motive Check

Bible Reading: Mark 11:24; 14:32-36

Key Verse: *He said, "Abba, Father, for you all things are possible; remove this cup from me; yet, not what I want, but what you want."* Mark 14:36, NRSV

Jesus, our example for prayer, once prayed, "Not what I want, but what you want." Often when we pray, we are motivated by our own interests and desires. We like to hear that we can have anything. But Jesus prayed with God's interests in mind (see Mark 14:36). When we pray, we are to express our desires, but we should want his will above ours. Check yourself to see if your prayers are focusing on your interests or on God's.

Unexpected Answers

Bible Reading: Acts 4:24-30

Key Verse: *Now, Lord, consider their threats and enable your servants to speak your word with great boldness.* Acts 4:29, NIV

Notice how the believers prayed. First, they praised God. Then they told God their specific problem and asked for his help. They did not ask God to remove the problem, but to help them deal with it. This is a model for us to follow when we pray. We may ask God to remove our problems, and he may choose to do so. But we must recognize that often God will leave the problem in place and give us the strength to deal with it.

How to Pray for Others

Bible Reading: Colossians 1:9-14

Key Verse: *For this reason, since the day we heard it, we have not ceased praying for you and asking that you may be filled*

*with the knowledge of God's will in all spiritual wisdom
and understanding.*   Colossians 1:9, NRSV

Sometimes we wonder how to pray for missionaries
and other leaders we have never met. Paul had never
met the Colossians, but he faithfully prayed for them.
His prayers teach us how to pray for others, whether we
know them or not. We can request that they (1) understand God's will, (2) gain spiritual wisdom, (3) live lives
pleasing and honoring to God, (4) do kind things for
others, (5) know God better and better, (6) would be
filled with God's strength, (7) endure in faith, (8) stay
full of Christ's joy, and (9) always be thankful. All believers have these same basic needs. When you don't know
how to pray for someone, remember Paul's prayer pattern for the Colossians.

What Happens When We Pray?

Bible Reading: 1 Thessalonians 5:9-18
Key Verse: *Pray without ceasing.*   1 Thessalonians 5:17, NKJV

Three things happen when we pray. First, we tell God
what is on our mind: our worries, joys, pains, fears,
hopes—everything. Nothing is too big or too trivial to
tell God. We can speak to him the way we would to our
most trusted friend.

Second, in prayer we can hear what God has to say to
us. Listening to God requires more patience and
practice than talking to him. Listening to God is one
more way he can give us guidance as we seek his will
(other ways include the Bible, the counsel of other
Christians, and knowing our own particular gifts and
limitations).

Third, when we pray, we come into God's presence.
Prayer brings us into God's throne room (Hebrews
4:16), where we may present our praise, confessions,
and requests.

As you pray, remember to thank God for the privilege
you have in coming to him. Remember also that
through prayer, we always have access to the one who

knows us, loves us, hears us, and is molding us into his
image.

CHECK IT OUT:

Genesis 3:1-7. *Without prayer, sin can come quickly.*
Nehemiah 1:4-11; 2:4; 4:4-5, 9; 5:19; 6:9; 13:14, 22, 29,
   31. *Nehemiah prayed in every situation.*
Psalm 3:4-5. *Praying to God gives rest and peace.*
Matthew 6:5-15. *Jesus teaches his disciples how to pray.*
Matthew 7:7-12. *Effective prayer takes persistence.*
Mark 1:35. *Jesus spent time in prayer.*
2 Thessalonians 1:11. *Pray for your friends.*
1 John 5:14-15. *God listens when we pray.*

PRIDE

Monuments to Yourself

Bible Reading: Genesis 11:1-9

Key Verse: *And they said, "Come, let us build for ourselves a city,
and a tower whose top will reach into heaven, and let us
make for ourselves a name; lest we be scattered abroad
over the face of the whole earth."*   Genesis 11:4, NASB

The Tower of Babel was a great human achievement, a
wonder of the world. But it was a monument to the
people themselves rather than to God. We often build
monuments to ourselves (a big house, a fancy car, or an
important career) to call attention to our achievements.
These may not be wrong in themselves, but when we
use them to give us identity and self-worth, they take
God's place in our lives. We are free to develop in many
areas, but we are not free to think we have replaced
God. What "monuments" are in your life?

Remember What God Has Given

Bible Reading: 2 Chronicles 26:11-23

Key Verse: *But after Uzziah became powerful, his pride led to his
downfall. He was unfaithful to the LORD his God, and*

*entered the temple of the LORD to burn incense on the
altar of incense.* 2 Chronicles 26:16, NIV

After God gave Uzziah great blessings and power, he
became proud and corrupt. It is true that "pride goes
before destruction" (Proverbs 16:18). Like Uzziah, we
sometimes take for granted what God has given us,
thinking we have made it ourselves. Of course, we have
put forth a lot of hard effort, but God supplied the
resources, gave us the abilities, and provided us with
the opportunities to make it happen. Instead of claiming our own greatness, we should proclaim God's greatness and give him the credit. Check your attitudes, and
use your gifts in ways that please him. If God has given
you money, influence, popularity, and power, be thankful and be careful. God hates pride.

Harmful Pride

Bible Reading: Jeremiah 13:12-17

Key Verse: *Hear and pay attention, do not be arrogant, for the LORD
has spoken.* Jeremiah 13:15, NIV

While it is good to respect our country and our church,
our loyalties always carry a hidden danger—pride.
When is pride harmful? When it causes us (1) to look
down on others; (2) to be selfish with our resources; (3)
to force our solutions on others' problems; (4) to think
God is blessing us because of our own merits; and (5) to
be content with our plans rather than seeking God's
plans.

Closed Ears

Bible Reading: Zephaniah 3:1-13

Key Verse: *She has not obeyed His voice, she has not received
correction; she has not trusted in the LORD, she has not
drawn near to her God.* Zephaniah 3:2, NKJV

Do you know people who refuse to listen when someone disagrees with their opinions? Those who are proud
often refuse to listen to anything that contradicts their
inflated self-esteem, and God's people had become so

proud that they would not hear or accept God's correction. Do you find it difficult to listen to the spiritual counsel of others or God's words from the Bible? You will be more willing to listen when you consider how weak and sinful you really are.

Passing Judgment

Bible Reading: 1 Corinthians 4:5-7

Key Verse: *Therefore do not go on passing judgment before the time, but wait until the Lord comes who will both bring to light the things hidden in the darkness and disclose the motives of men's hearts; and then each man's praise will come to him from God.* 1 Corinthians 4:5, NASB

It is tempting to judge a fellow Christian, evaluating whether or not he or she is a good follower of Christ. But only God knows a person's heart, and he is the only one with the right to judge. Paul's warning to the Corinthians should also warn us. We should help those who are sinning (see 5:12-13), but we must not judge who is a better servant of Christ. When you judge someone, you automatically consider yourself better, and that is pride.

Don't Let Pride Get in the Way

Bible Reading: 2 Corinthians 7:8-12

Key Verse: *For see what earnestness this godly grief has produced in you, what eagerness to clear yourselves, what indignation, what alarm, what longing, what zeal, what punishment! At every point you have proved yourselves guiltless in the matter.* 2 Corinthians 7:11, NRSV

Paul knew that it was difficult for people to hear that they had sinned, and even more difficult to get rid of sin. That is why he praised the Corinthians for clearing up an especially troublesome situation. How do you respond to confrontation? Do you tend to be defensive? Don't let pride keep you from admitting your sins. Accept confrontation as a tool for growth, and do all you can to correct problems that are pointed out to you.

CHECK IT OUT:

> 2 Kings 19:23-29. *Never take credit for what God has done.*
> Proverbs 6:16-17. *God hates pride.*
> Proverbs 11:2. *Pride ends in shame.*
> Proverbs 13:10. *Pride starts arguments and ruins friendships.*
> Proverbs 16:5. *Pride leads to punishment.*
> Proverbs 18:12. *Pride ends in destruction.*
> Proverbs 29:23. *Pride ends in a fall.*
> Daniel 4:19-32. *Nebuchadnezzar was a victim of pride.*
> Matthew 11:20-26. *Pride keeps people from finding Christ.*
> Acts 12:19-23. *Herod was another victim of pride.*
> 1 John 2:15-17. *Pride is not from God.*
>
> *(see also Self-Centeredness)*

PRIORITIES
(SEE VALUES)

PROBLEMS

Don't Run Away

Bible Reading: Genesis 16:1-16

Key Verse: *And He said, "Hagar, Sarai's maid, where have you come from, and where are you going?" She said, "I am fleeing from the presence of my mistress Sarai."*

Genesis 16:8, NKJV

As Hagar was running away from her mistress and her problem, the angel of the Lord gave her this advice: Return and face Sarai (the cause of her problem) and act as you should. Hagar needed to work on her attitude toward Sarai, no matter how justified it may have been. Running away from our problems rarely solves them. It is wise to face our problems squarely, accept God's promise of help, correct our attitudes, and act as we should.

Prevail over Problems

Bible Reading: Genesis 35:9-15

Key Verse: *God said to him, "Your name is Jacob, but you will no longer be called Jacob; your name will be Israel." So he named him Israel.* Genesis 35:10, NIV

God reminded Jacob of his new name, Israel, which meant "he struggles with God." Although Jacob's life was littered with difficulties and trials, his new name was a tribute to his desire to stay close to God despite life's disappointments.

Many people believe that Christianity should offer a problem-free life. Consequently, as life gets tough, they draw back disappointed. Instead, they should determine to stick close to God through life's storms. Problems and difficulties are painful but inevitable. You might as well see them as opportunities for growth. You can't prevail with God unless you have troubles to prevail over.

Keep Your Perspective

Bible Reading: Exodus 16:1-3

Key Verse: *The whole congregation of the Israelites complained against Moses and Aaron in the wilderness.* Exodus 16:2, NRSV

It happened again. As the Israelites encountered danger, shortages, and inconvenience, they complained bitterly and longed to be back in Egypt. But, as always, God provided for their needs. Difficult circumstances often lead to stress, and complaining is a natural response. The Israelites didn't really want to be slaves back in Egypt—they just wanted life to get a little easier. In the middle of their problems, they could not focus on the cause of their stress (in this case, lack of trust in God). They could only think about the quickest way of escape. When pressure comes your way, resist the temptation to make a quick escape. Instead, focus on God's power and wisdom to help you deal with the problem.

Rely on God

Bible Reading: 1 Samuel 14:1-23

Key Verse: *Jonathan said to his young armor-bearer, "Come, let's go over to the outpost of those uncircumcised fellows. Perhaps the LORD will act in our behalf. Nothing can hinder the LORD from saving, whether by many or by few."*   1 Samuel 14:6, NIV

Jonathan and his bodyguard weren't much of a force to attack the huge Philistine army. But while everyone else was afraid, they trusted God, knowing that the size of the enemy army had no relationship to God's ability to help them. God honored the faith and brave action of these two men with a tremendous victory.

Have you ever felt surrounded by the "enemy" or faced overwhelming odds? God is never intimidated by the size of the enemy or the complexity of a problem. With him, there are always enough resources to resist the pressures and win your battles. If God has called you to action, then bravely commit what few resources you have to God, and rely upon him to give you the victory.

Do What You Can and Leave the Rest to God

Bible Reading: 2 Chronicles 32:1-22

Key Verse: *Be strong and of good courage. Do not be afraid or dismayed before the king of Assyria and all the horde that is with him; for there is one greater with us than with him.*   2 Chronicles 32:7, NRSV

When King Hezekiah was confronted with the frightening prospect of an Assyrian invasion, he made two important decisions. He did everything he could to deal with the situation, and he trusted God for the outcome. That is exactly what we must do when we face difficult or frightening situations. Do everything you possibly can to solve the problem or improve the situation. As you do this, commit it to God in prayer, and trust him for the solution.

Problems Can Help Us

Bible Reading: Psalm 106:34-48

Key Verse: *Save us, O LORD our God, and gather us from among the nations, that we may give thanks to your holy name and glory in your praise.* Psalm 106:47, NRSV

God allowed trouble to come to the Israelites in order to help them. Our troubles can be helpful because they (1) humble us, (2) pull us from the allurements of the world and drive us back to God, (3) quicken our prayers, (4) allow us to experience more of God's faithfulness, (5) make us more dependent upon God, (6) encourage us to submit to God's purpose for our lives, and (7) make us more compassionate to others in trouble.

Renew Your Strength

Bible Reading: Isaiah 40:25-31

Key Verse: *But those who wait on the Lord shall renew their strength; they shall mount up with wings like eagles, they shall run and not be weary, they shall walk and not faint.* Isaiah 40:31, NKJV

Even the strongest people get tired at times, but God's power and strength never diminish. He is never too tired or too busy to help and listen. His strength is our source of strength. When you feel all of life crushing you and you cannot go another step, remember that you can call upon God to renew your strength.

Part of God's Plan

Bible Reading: 2 Thessalonians 1:1-10

Key Verse: *All this is evidence that God's judgment is right, and as a result you will be counted worthy of the kingdom of God, for which you are suffering.* 2 Thessalonians 1:5, NIV

As we live for Christ, we will experience troubles and hardships. Some say that troubles are a result of sin or lack of faith, but Paul teaches that they may be a part of God's plan for believers. Our problems help us look upward and forward, not inward (Mark 13:35-36); they help build strong character (Romans 5:3-4); and they help us to be sensitive to others who also must struggle (2 Corinthians 1:3-5).

Getting through the Rough Times

Bible Reading: James 1:2-8

Key Verse: *But let patience have its perfect work, that you may be perfect and complete, lacking nothing.* James 1:4, NKJV

We can't really know the depth of our character until we see how we react under pressure. It is easy to be kind when everything is going well, but can we still be kind when others are treating us unfairly? Instead of complaining about our struggles, we should see them as opportunities for growth. Thank God for promising to be with you in rough times. Ask him to help you solve your problems or give you the strength to endure them. Then be patient. God will not leave you alone with your problems. He will stay close by and help you grow.

CHECK IT OUT:

Deuteronomy 29:29. *Trust God whether you understand your troubles or not.*

Psalm 3. *God is our hope in troubles.*

Matthew 11:28-30. *God gives you rest from your troubles.*

Romans 8:28. *God can bring good from any problem.*

2 Corinthians 1:3-5. *When you're facing troubles, help others who are also in need.*

2 Corinthians 4:8-18; 6:3-10; 11:23-33. *Don't give up.*

Philippians 1:29-30. *Be willing to suffer for the Good News of Christ.*

Philippians 3:7-11. *Suffering can bring you closer to God.*

Colossians 2:6-7. *Trust Christ for each day's problems.*

James 1:2-4. *Be happy when facing difficult trials.*

(see also Depression, Discouragement, and Failure)

PURITY

Sexual Purity

Bible Reading: Song of Songs 4:8-15

Key Verse: *You are a garden locked up, my sister, my bride; you are a spring enclosed, a sealed fountain.*

Song of Songs 4:12, NIV

In comparing his bride to a private garden, Solomon was praising her virginity. Virginity, considered old-fashioned by many in today's culture, has always been God's plan for unmarried people—and with good reason. Sex without marriage is cheap. It cannot compare with the joy of giving yourself completely to the one who is totally committed to you.

Purity in a Polluted World

Bible Reading: Ezekiel 20:30-38

Key Verse: *Therefore say to the house of Israel: "This is what the Sovereign LORD says: Will you defile yourselves the way your fathers did and lust after their vile images?"*

Ezekiel 20:30, NIV

Water containing contaminants is polluted. Likewise, our lives are polluted when we accept the contaminants—immoral values—of this world. If we love money, we become greedy. If we lust, we become sexually immoral. Remaining pure in a polluted world is difficult, to say the least. But a heart filled with God's Holy Spirit leaves little room for pollution (see Titus 1:15-16).

Why Try to Stay Pure?

Bible Reading: 1 Timothy 3:16; 6:11-16

Key Verse: *But you, O man of God, flee these things and pursue righteousness, godliness, faith, love, patience, gentleness.*

1 Timothy 6:11, NKJV

Trying to stay pure and not sin seems like a full-time job, and sometimes we wonder why we even should bother. After all, no one else seems to. But Jesus makes it clear that we are to be pure. While Jesus wants us to have pure thoughts and actions, there's a lot more to it. Anybody can be (or seem) pure on the outside, at least for a while. But Jesus wants purity on the inside. This begins by accepting Christ's death on the cross as punishment for our sins. When we do this, we take on Christ's goodness, and, in God's eyes, we are pure and destined to spend eternity in heaven!

It doesn't stop there, of course. God wants us to be like Jesus, and this is a lifetime process of allowing him to change and mold us. This can only happen by staying close to Christ and living like he wants us to. When we do this, we will not only grow as Christians but remain pure. These two things are natural by-products of staying close to Christ.

CHECK IT OUT:

Psalm 1:1-3. *A pure life brings blessings.*

Psalm 119:1-20. *Living by God's Word will help you stay pure.*

Matthew 5:27-30. *Purity starts in the heart.*

Matthew 23:13-26. *Real purity isn't for show.*

Philippians 3:7-11. *Give up what hinders purity.*

Philippians 4:8. *Keep your thoughts pure.*

1 Thessalonians 4:1-8. *God wants you to be pure.*

Titus 1:15. *A pure person sees goodness in all things.*

(see also Sex/Sexual Sin)

REJECTION

God Can Use You

Bible Reading: Judges 11:1-11

Key Verse: *Then Jephthah said to the elders of Gilead, "Did you not hate me and drive me from my father's house? So why have you come to me now when you are in trouble?"*
Judges 11:7, NASB

Jephthah, an illegitimate son of Gilead, was chased out of the country by his half brothers. He suffered as a result of another person's decision and not for any wrong he had done. Yet in spite of his brothers' rejection, God used him. If you are suffering from unfair rejection, don't blame others and become discouraged. Remember how God used Jephthah despite his unjust circumstances, and realize that God is able to use you even if you have been rejected.

Don't Give Up

Bible Reading: Jeremiah 25:2-7

Key Verse: *Yet you did not listen to me, says the LORD, and so you have provoked me to anger with the work of your hands to your own harm.* Jeremiah 25:7, NRSV

Imagine preaching the same message for twenty-three years and continually being rejected! Jeremiah faced this, but because he had committed his life to God, he continued to proclaim the message, "Turn from your evil ways." Regardless of the people's response, Jeremiah did not give up. God never stops loving us, even when we reject him. We can thank God that he won't give up on us, and, like Jeremiah, we can commit ourselves to never giving God up. No matter how people respond when you tell them about God, remain faithful to his high call and continue to witness for him.

You're in Good Company

Bible Reading: Acts 5:12-42

Key Verse: *But the high priest rose up, along with all his associates (that is the sect of the Sadducees), and they were filled with jealousy.* Acts 5:17, NASB

The apostles had power to do miracles, great boldness in preaching, and God's presence in their lives. Yet they were not free from hatred and persecution. They were arrested and put in jail, beaten with rods and whips, and slandered by community leaders.

Faith in God does not make troubles disappear. Rather, it makes troubles appear less fearsome because it puts them in the right perspective. You cannot expect everyone to react favorably when you share something as dynamic as your faith in Christ. But remember that you must be more concerned about God's reactions than people's.

Doing Something Right

Bible Reading: Acts 13:42-52

Key Verse: *But the Jews stirred up the devout and prominent women and the chief men of the city, raised up persecution against Paul and Barnabas, and expelled them from their region.* Acts 13:50, NKJV

It is not shameful to suffer for being a Christian. When Paul and Barnabas were persecuted for preaching the Good News, they went on to the next town. When you suffer or are rejected for your faith in God, don't be discouraged. Persecution may be a mark of God's approval of your faith. Don't seek out suffering, but don't try to avoid it. Instead, keep on doing what is right regardless of the suffering it might bring.

People are watching you and other Christians at your school or office. They are seeing how you respond to rejection and verbal abuse. Within those crowded halls are people who want to believe in something true, something worth living for no matter what the cost. And when they find it, they may make an incredible impact in their world for Christ.

What do they learn from watching you?

CHECK IT OUT:

Isaiah 53:1-9. *Jesus' rejection is foretold.*

Matthew 13:53-58. *A prophet is rejected in his hometown.*

Luke 15:11-24. *God will never reject repentant sinners.*

John 6:58-66. *Jesus knows how rejection feels.*

John 15:17-21. *Jesus warned the disciples to expect rejection.*

Romans 1:18-32. *Rejecting God allows sin to run wild.*

REPENTANCE

A Fresh Start

Bible Reading: Deuteronomy 30:1-20

Key Verse: *And the LORD your God will circumcise your heart and the heart of your descendants, to love the LORD your God with all your heart and with all your soul, that you may live.* Deuteronomy 30:6, NKJV

Moses told the Hebrews that when they were ready to return to God, he would be ready to receive them. God's mercy is unbelievable. It goes far beyond what we can imagine. Even if the Jews deliberately walked away from him and ruined their lives, God would still take them back. God wants to forgive us and bring us back to himself, too. Some people will not learn this until their world has crashed in around them. Then the sorrow and pain seem to open their eyes to what God has been saying all along. Are you separated from God by sin? No matter how far you have wandered, God promises a fresh beginning if only you will turn to him.

How to Truly Repent

Bible Reading: 2 Chronicles 7:11-22

Key Verse: *If my people, who are called by my name, will humble themselves and pray and seek my face and turn from their wicked ways, then will I hear from heaven and will forgive their sin and will heal their land.*

2 Chronicles 7:14, NIV

In chapter 6, Solomon asked God to make provisions for the people when they sinned. God answered with four conditions for forgiveness: (1) Humble yourself by admitting your sins; (2) pray to God, asking for forgiveness; (3) search for God continually; and (4) turn from sinful habits. True repentance is more than talk—it is changed behavior. Whether we sin individually, as a group, or as a nation, following these steps will lead to forgiveness.

God Listens to Our Intentions

Bible Reading: Proverbs 28:1-14

Key Verse: *When one will not listen to the law, even one's prayers are an abomination.* Proverbs 28:9, NRSV

God does not listen to our prayers if we intend to go back to our sin as soon as we get off our knees. If we want to forsake our sin and follow him, however, he willingly listens—no matter how bad our sin has been. What closes his ears is not the depth of our sin, but our intention to do it again.

Repenting Means Changing

Bible Reading: Hosea 6:1-11

Key Verse: *For I desire mercy and not sacrifice, and the knowledge of God more than burnt offerings.* Hosea 6:6, NKJV

Israel was interested in God only for the material benefits he provided—they did not value the eternal benefits that come from worshiping him. Theirs was far from genuine repentance because they did not turn from idols, pledge to change, or regret their sins. They thought God's wrath would last only a few days. Little did they know that their nation would soon be taken into exile.

Before judging these people, however, consider *your* attitude. What do you hope to gain from your religion? Do you "repent" easily, without seriously considering what changes need to take place in your life? Don't treat your relationship with God carelessly.

Refreshment from God

Bible Reading: Acts 3:12-26

Key Verse: *Repent therefore, and turn to God so that your sins may be wiped out.* Acts 3:19, NRSV

When we repent, God promises not only to wipe away our sin, but also to bring spiritual refreshment. Repentance may at first seem painful because it is hard to give up certain sins. But God will give you a better way. As Hosea promised, "Let us know, let us press on to know the LORD; his appearing is as sure as the dawn; he will come to us like the showers, like the spring rains that water the earth" (Hosea 6:3, NRSV). Do you feel a need to be refreshed?

CHECK IT OUT:

> Jonah 3:10. *A great city repents.*
> Mark 1:14-15. *Repentance was the focus of Jesus' message.*
> Acts 3:19. *Repent so God can clear away your sins.*
> 2 Corinthians 7:10. *Grief can bring repentance.*
> 1 John 1:8-10. *If we confess and repent, God will forgive.*

(see also Confession and Forgiveness)

REPUTATION

Getting Past Your Past

Bible Reading: Joshua 2:1-21

Key Verse: *When we heard of it, our hearts melted and everyone's courage failed because of you, for the LORD your God is God in heaven above and on the earth below.*
Joshua 2:11, NIV

Why would the spies stop at the house of Rahab the prostitute? Several reasons: (1) It was a good place to gather information and have no questions asked in return; (2) Rahab's house was in an ideal location for a quick escape because it was built into the city wall; and (3) God directed the spies to Rahab's house because he knew her heart was open to him and that she would be instrumental in the Israelite victory over Jericho. God often uses people with simple faith to accomplish his great purposes, no matter what kind of past they have had or how insignificant they seem to be. Rahab didn't allow her past to keep her from the new role God had for her.

What Will You Leave Behind?

Bible Reading: 1 Chronicles 2:1-7

Key Verse: *Now Er, Judah's firstborn, was wicked in the sight of the* LORD, *and he put him to death.*   1 Chronicles 2:3, NRSV

This long genealogy not only lists names, but also gives us insights into some of the people. Here, almost as an epitaph, the genealogy states that Er was so wicked that the Lord killed him. Now, centuries later, this is all we know of the man.

Like Er, each of us is forging a reputation, developing personal qualities by which we will be remembered. How would God summarize your life up to now? Some defiantly claim that how they live is their own business. But Scripture teaches that the way you live today will determine how you will be remembered by others and how you will be judged by God. What you do now *does* matter.

Well Remembered

Bible Reading: Mark 15:42-47

Key Verse: *Joseph of Arimathea, a prominent member of the Council, who was himself waiting for the kingdom of God, went boldly to Pilate and asked for Jesus' body.*
Mark 15:43, NIV

After Jesus died on the cross, Joseph of Arimathea asked for his body and then sealed it in a new tomb. By doing so, Joseph was risking his reputation as an honored member of the Jewish Supreme Court to give a proper burial to the one he followed. It is frightening to risk one's reputation even for what is right. If your Christian witness endangers your reputation, consider Joseph.

Today he is well known in the Christian church. How many of the other members of the Jewish Supreme Court can you name?

CHECK IT OUT:

Ruth 2:1-13. *Integrity builds a good reputation.*

Psalm 38:12-16. *Hate sin and God will protect your reputation.*

Ecclesiastes 7:1. *A good reputation has great value.*

John 7:50-51. *Risk your reputation for Christ.*

2 Corinthians 12:11-18. *Stand up for your reputation.*

Titus 1:5-9. *Your reputation reflects your lifestyle.*

Hebrews 11. *People of strong faith have a lasting reputation.*

RESPONSIBILITY

See It Through

Bible Reading: Genesis 43:1-14

Key Verse: *I myself will guarantee his safety; you can hold me personally responsible for him.* Genesis 43:9, NIV

Judah accepted full responsibility for Benjamin's safety. He did not know what that might mean for him, but he was determined to carry it out. In the end it was Judah's stirring words that caused Joseph to break down and reveal himself to his brothers (44:18-34). Accepting and fulfilling responsibilities is difficult, but it builds character and confidence, earns others' respect, and motivates us to complete our work. When you have been given an assignment to complete or a responsibility to fulfill, commit yourself to seeing it through.

Making Restitution

Bible Reading: Exodus 22:1-15

Key Verse: *If a man steals an ox or a sheep, and slaughters it or sells it, he shall restore five oxen for an ox and four sheep for a sheep.* Exodus 22:1, NKJV

Throughout chapter 22 we find examples of the principle of restitution—making wrongs right. For example, if a man stole an animal, he had to repay double the beast's market value. If you have done someone wrong, perhaps you should go beyond what is expected to make things right. This will (1) help ease any pain you've caused, (2) help the other person be more forgiving, and (3) make you more likely to think before you do it again.

Don't Run

Bible Reading: 1 Samuel 10:17-27

Key Verse: *Therefore they inquired further of the LORD, "Has the man come here yet?" So the LORD said, "Behold, he is hiding himself by the baggage."* 1 Samuel 10:22, NASB

When the king was to be chosen, Saul already knew that he was the one (10:1). Instead of coming forward, however, he hid in the baggage. Often we hide from important responsibilities because we are afraid of failure, afraid of what others will think, or perhaps unsure about how to proceed. Don't run from your responsibilities.

In Training

Bible Reading: Psalm 78:52-72

Key Verse: *From tending the sheep he brought him to be the shepherd of his people Jacob, of Israel his inheritance.* Psalm 78:71, NIV

Although David had been on the throne when this psalm was written, he is called a shepherd and not a king. Shepherding, a common profession in biblical times, was a highly responsible job. The flocks were completely dependent upon shepherds for guidance, provision, and protection. David had spent his early years as a shepherd (1 Samuel 16:10-11). This was a training ground for the future responsibilities God had in store for him. When he was ready, God took him from caring for sheep to caring for Israel, God's people. Don't treat your present situation lightly or irresponsibly. It may be God's training ground for your future.

CHECK IT OUT:

> Genesis 1:28-30. *God has given us a responsibility to care for the earth.*
> Joshua 1:5-9. *When you face big responsibilities, be encouraged that God is with you.*
> 1 Chronicles 21:8. *Take responsibility when you do wrong.*
> Matthew 5:13-16. *Christians are responsible to light up a dark world.*
> Matthew 25:14-30. *We should use what we have responsibly.*
> Matthew 27:23-26. *God holds us accountable.*
> 1 Timothy 3:1-16. *Leaders have strict responsibilities.*

REVENGE

Restoration, Not Revenge

Bible Reading: Numbers 5:5-10

Key Verse: *The person shall make full restitution for the wrong, adding one fifth to it, and giving it to the one who was wronged.* Numbers 5:7, NRSV

God included restitution, a unique concept for that day, as part of his law for Israel. When someone was robbed, the guilty person was required to restore to the victim what had been taken and pay an additional interest penalty. When we have wronged others, we should look for ways to set things right and, if possible, leave the victim even better off than when we harmed him or her. When we have been wronged, we should still seek restoration rather than striking out in revenge.

God's Justice

Bible Reading: Numbers 16:1-22

Key Verse: *But Moses and Aaron fell facedown and cried out, "O God, God of the spirits of all mankind, will you be angry with the entire assembly when only one man sins?"* Numbers 16:22, NIV

Moses and Aaron prayed for those with whom they were most angry and frustrated. Do you pray for those who try to hurt you? Or do you seek revenge, asking God to help you get even? Only those who have a deep relationship with God understand that he will settle the score with those who rebel. It is not our job to seek revenge against those who wrong us. God will make certain that, in the end, justice is done.

Endless Cycle

Bible Reading: Judges 15:1-11

Key Verse: *And he said to them, "As they did to me, so I have done to them."* Judges 15:11, NKJV

Why is seeking revenge so harmful? Samson's reply tells the story: "As they did to me, so I have done to them." Revenge is an uncontrollable monster. Each act of retaliation brings another. It is a boomerang that cannot be thrown without cost to the thrower. The revenge cycle can be halted only by forgiveness.

Facing Slander

Bible Reading: Psalm 7:1-17

Key Verse: *Arise, O LORD, in your anger; rise up against the rage of my enemies. Awake, my God; decree justice.*
Psalm 7:6, NIV

Have you ever been falsely accused or badly hurt and wanted revenge? David wrote this psalm in response to the slanderous accusations of those who claimed that he was trying to kill King Saul and seize the throne (1 Samuel 24:9-11). Instead of seeking revenge, David cried out to God for justice. The proper response to slander is prayer, not revenge. God says, "Justice belongs to me; I will repay them" (Deuteronomy 32:35-36; Hebrews 10:30). The next time you are slandered, ask God to take your case, bring justice, and restore your reputation.

Rise above Revenge

Bible Reading: 1 Peter 3:8-17

Key Verse: *Do not repay evil for evil or abuse for abuse; but, on the contrary, repay with a blessing.*   1 Peter 3:9, NRSV

In our sinful world, it is often acceptable to tear people down verbally or get back at them if we feel hurt. Remembering Jesus' teaching to turn the other cheek (Matthew 5:39), Peter encourages his readers to pay back wrongs by praying for the offenders. In God's kingdom, taking revenge and insulting a person, no matter how indirectly done, are unacceptable behaviors. Rise above getting back at those who hurt you. Instead of reacting angrily to those people, pray for them.

CHECK IT OUT:

Judges 15:1-15. *Revenge can become a habit.*
Psalm 35:1-10. *Let God fight your battles for you.*
Matthew 5:38-48. *Christians should pay back evil with good.*
Romans 12:19. *Leave vengeance to God.*
1 Peter 3:8-9. *Be tender and humble.*

(see also Anger)

SALVATION

You Can't Inherit Salvation

Bible Reading: Luke 3:1-18

Key Verse: *Produce fruit in keeping with repentance. And do not begin to say to yourselves, "We have Abraham as our father.' For I tell you that out of these stones God can raise up children for Abraham.* Luke 3:8, NIV

In Jesus' day, the religious leaders relied more on their family line than on their faith for their standing with God. That's why many of John's hearers were shocked when he said that being Abraham's descendants was not enough. But a relationship with God is not handed down from parents to children. Everyone has to develop a relationship with God on his or her own. Don't rely on someone else for your salvation. Put your faith in Jesus, and then exercise your faith by acting on it every day.

How You Can Be Saved

Bible Reading: Romans 10:8-13

Key Verse: *For "whoever calls on the name of the LORD shall be saved."* Romans 10:13, NKJV

Have you ever been asked, "How do I become a Christian?" These verses give you the beautiful answer—salvation is as close as your own heart and mouth. People think it must be a complicated process, but it is not. If you believe in your heart and say with your mouth that Christ is the risen Lord, you will be saved.

A Free Gift

Bible Reading: Romans 11:1-6

Key Verse: *But if it is by grace, it is no longer on the basis of works, otherwise grace is no longer grace.* Romans 11:6, NASB

This great truth can be hard to grasp. Do you think it's easier for God to love you when you're good? Do you secretly suspect God chose you because you deserved to be chosen? Do you think some people's behavior is so bad that God couldn't possibly save them? If you think this way, you don't entirely understand the Good News—salvation is a free gift. It cannot be earned, in whole or in part. It can only be accepted with thankfulness and praise.

You Can't Earn Salvation

Bible Reading: 1 Corinthians 1:26-31

Key Verse: *It is because of him that you are in Christ Jesus, who has become for us wisdom from God—that is, our righteousness, holiness and redemption.*

1 Corinthians 1:30, NIV

Paul emphasizes that the way to receive salvation is so ordinary and simple that *any* person who wants to can understand it. Skill does not get you into God's kingdom—simple faith does. God planned it this way so no one could boast that his or her achievements helped him or her secure eternal life. Salvation is totally from God through Jesus' death, which allowed us to become perfect in God's eyes. There is *nothing* we can do to become acceptable to God. We need only accept what Jesus has already done for us.

God's Chosen

Bible Reading: Ephesians 1:3-14

Key Verse: *He chose us in Him before the foundation of the world, that we should be holy and without blame before Him in love.* Ephesians 1:4, NKJV

Paul said, "[God] chose us," to emphasize that salvation depends totally on God. We are not saved because we deserve it, but because God is gracious and freely gives it. We did not influence God's decision to save us. He did it according to his plan. The mystery of salvation originated in the timeless mind of God long before we existed. Thus there is no way to take credit for your salvation or to find room for pride. It is hard to understand how God could accept us, but because of Christ we are holy and blameless in his eyes. God chose you, and when you belong to him through Jesus Christ, he looks at you as if you had never sinned.

Christ Paid the Price

Bible Reading: Hebrews 7:24-28; 9:25-26

Key Verse: *Consequently he is able for all time to save those who approach God through him, since he always lives to make intercession for them.* Hebrews 7:25, NRSV

What does it mean that Jesus is "able for all time to save"? No one else can add to what Jesus did to save us. Our past, present, and future sins are all forgiven, and Jesus is with the Father as a sign that our sins are forgiven. If you are a Christian, remember that Christ has paid the price for your sins once and for all.

CHECK IT OUT:

Matthew 8:18-22. *Be totally committed to Christ.*
Matthew 19:25-26. *Salvation is by God's grace alone.*
John 3:16. *Jesus is God's plan for salvation.*
John 10:10. *God wants to give us life in its fullness.*
Romans 3:23. *No one deserves salvation.*
Romans 6:23. *God's penalty for sin is death.*
Romans 8:38-39. *Salvation is eternal.*
Romans 10:9-10. *Paul explains how to be saved.*
Ephesians 2:8-9. *God gives salvation as a gift.*
Philippians 3:4-11. *No one is good enough to be saved.*

SELF-CENTEREDNESS

Trying to Get It All

Bible Reading: 2 Chronicles 10:1-19

Key Verse: *[Rehoboam] followed the advice of the young men and said, "My father made your yoke heavy; I will make it*

even heavier. My father scourged you with whips; I will scourge you with scorpions." 2 Chronicles 10:14, NIV

In trying to have it all, Rehoboam lost almost everything. Motivated by greed and power, he pressed too hard and caused his kingdom to be divided. He didn't need more money or power, because he had inherited the richest kingdom in the world. He didn't need more control because the land had peace. His demands were based on selfishness rather than reason or spiritual discernment. Those who insist on having it all often wind up with little or nothing. We must temper our stubborn selfishness by putting God first in our lives, acknowledging that he knows what is best for us, and living his way.

The Power of Pride

Bible Reading: Obadiah 1:1-21

Key Verse: *Your proud heart has deceived you, you that live in the clefts of the rock, whose dwelling is in the heights. You say in your heart, "Who will bring me down to the ground?"* Obadiah 1:3, NRSV

Edom was destroyed because of her pride. Pride destroys individuals as well as nations. It makes us think we can take care of ourselves without God's help. But even serving God and others can lead us into pride. Take inventory of your life and service for God, asking him to point out and remove any pride.

Trying to Impress

Bible Reading: Luke 14:7-24

Key Verse: *But when you are invited, take the lowest place, so that when your host comes, he will say to you, "Friend, move up to a better place." Then you will be honored in the presence of all your fellow guests.* Luke 14:10, NIV

Jesus advised people not to rush for the best seats at a feast. People today are just as eager to raise their social status, whether by being with the right people, dressing for success, or driving the right car. Wanting a nice car or hoping to be successful in your career is not wrong in itself—it is wrong only when you want these things just to impress others. Whom do you try to impress? Rather than aiming for prestige, look for a place where you can serve. If God wants you to serve on a wider scale, he will invite you to take a higher place.

CHECK IT OUT:

Genesis 13:8-9. *Abraham shows consideration for others.*
Matthew 10:39. *Don't try to hold back part of your life from God.*
Matthew 19:13-15. *Never be so self-centered that you can't be kind to children.*
John 6:38. *Christ is our example.*
1 Corinthians 10:24. *Don't just think about yourself.*
1 Corinthians 13:4-5. *Paul defines what love is and isn't.*
Philippians 3:7-11. *Focus on Christ.*

(see also Humility and Pride)

SERVING OTHERS
(SEE CARING FOR OTHERS)

SEX/SEXUAL SIN

Sinful Seduction

Bible Reading: Genesis 39:1-23

Key Verse: *There is no one greater in this house than I, and he has withheld nothing from me except you, because you are his wife. How then could I do this great evil, and sin against God?*
　　　　　　　　　　　　　　　　Genesis 39:9, NASB

Potiphar's wife failed to seduce Joseph, who resisted this temptation by saying it would be a sin against God. Joseph didn't say, "I'd be hurting you," or "I'd be sinning against Potiphar," or "I'd be sinning against myself." Under pressure, such excuses are easily rationalized away. Remember that sexual sin is not just between two consenting adults. It is an act of disobedience against God.

Sex Can Destroy

Bible Reading: Deuteronomy 23:17-18

Key Verse: *No Israelite man or woman is to become a shrine prostitute.* Deuteronomy 23:17, NIV

Prostitution was strictly forbidden. To forbid this practice may seem obvious to us, but it may not have been so obvious to the Israelites. Almost every other religion known to them included prostitution as an important part of its worship services. Prostitution makes a mockery of God's original idea for sex. It treats sex as an isolated physical act rather than an act of commitment to another. Outside of marriage, sex destroys relationships. Within marriage, if approached with the right attitude, it can be a relationship builder. God frequently had to warn the Israelites against the practice of extramarital sex. Today we still need to hear his warnings. Single people need to be warned about premarital sex, and married people need to be warned about sexual infidelity.

Watch Out for Temptation

Bible Reading: Judges 8:28-32; 9:1-6

Key Verse: *His concubine who was in Shechem also bore him a son, and he named him Abimelech.* Judges 8:31, NRSV

This relationship between Gideon and a concubine produced a son who tore apart Gideon's family and caused tragedy for the nation. Gideon's story illustrates the fact that heroes in battle are not always heroes in daily life. Gideon led the nation but could not lead his family. No matter who you are, moral laxness will cause problems. Just because you have won a single battle with temptation does not mean you will automatically win the next. We need to be constantly watchful against temptation. Sometimes Satan's strongest attacks come after a victory.

Lust Is Not Love

Bible Reading: 2 Samuel 13:1-20

Key Verse: *Then Amnon was seized with a very great loathing for her; indeed, his loathing was even greater than the lust he had felt for her. Amnon said to her, "Get out!"*

2 Samuel 13:15, NRSV

Amnon may have been a victim of "love at first sight," but his actions were impulsive and evil. Because he was actually overcome by lust, his so-called love turned to hatred after he raped Tamar. But his destructive actions hurt not only Tamar but also his entire family (13:21-31). The consequences of his deed were severe for everyone involved. Nothing could excuse the evil he did by raping his sister. Don't allow sexual passion to boil over into evil actions. Passion must be controlled.

The Problem with Pornography

Bible Reading: Job 31:1-12; Matthew 5:27-30

Key Verse: *I made a covenant with my eyes not to look lustfully at a girl.*

Job 31:1, NIV

Job had the right idea when he made this covenant. Unfortunately, many men don't follow his example. Some limit their involvement in this sin by just looking at other women lustfully. Others, however, go one step farther and get into pornography.

The problem with pornography is that what is portrayed is evil and against God's commands. It is a lie, for it takes away from the true beauty of sex that exists between two people who are married and committed to each other for life. Pornography twists what God intended as a joyful part of marriage into something sick, perverse, and evil. On top of that, pornography is addictive. Like an alcoholic who needs harder liquor to get that "buzz," those addicted to pornography will soon need to move on to harder porn. It becomes an obsession, and it can lead to committing grotesquely perverted sinful acts that produce incredible guilt. Don't think that just because you're a Christian, you're immune. If you're into porn, get out now. Talk to someone you trust, and get help, advice, and support in kicking the habit. Pray regularly. You can kick the habit with God's help.

When Is Sex Right?

Bible Reading: Hebrews 13:4

Key Verse: *Marriage should be honored by all, and the marriage bed kept pure, for God will judge the adulterer and all the sexually immoral.* Hebrews 13:4, NIV

Contrary to what you might think, sex wasn't created by music videos or porn magazines. God himself created sex; therefore sex is good. The problem is that people haven't followed God's guidelines for sex and have turned sex into something perverse, selfish, even evil. Three facts are clear: (1) *Sex is good.* Within the bounds of marriage, sex is part of God's plan for building a marriage relationship and for creating children. (2) *Sex is powerful.* Of all the ways people can express love for each other, sex is the most powerful because it involves each person's total being. Within marriage, it is a beautiful act of union and oneness. Outside of marriage, it is incredibly destructive. (3) *Sex is made for marriage alone.* Because of its goodness and its power, God purposely placed it within the confines of a relationship that is loving, supportive, and committed. Because sex is 100 percent physical commitment, it needs an environment of 100 percent emotional, social, and spiritual commitment.

Don't shortchange yourself with cheap thrills that can lead only to pain, anger, and shame. If you follow God's plan—including waiting until marriage to have sex—you'll experience one of God's greatest gifts in a way that is fulfilling to you and your spouse, leading to deeper love for each other.

When Is Sex Wrong?

Bible Reading: Revelation 2:20-23

Key Verse: *Nevertheless I have a few things against you, because you allow that woman Jezebel, who calls herself a*

*prophetess, to teach and seduce My servants to commit
sexual immorality and eat things sacrificed to idols.*

Revelation 2:20, NKJV

Why is sexual sin serious? Sex outside marriage always
hurts someone. It hurts God because it shows that we
prefer to follow our own desires instead of God's Word.
It hurts others because it violates the commitment so
necessary to a relationship. It hurts us because it often
brings disease to our bodies and harms our personali-
ties. In addition, sexual sin has tremendous power to
destroy families, communities, and even nations
because it destroys the relationships upon which these
institutions are built. God wants to protect us from
hurting ourselves and others, so we should have no
part in sexual sin, even if our society says it's all right.

CHECK IT OUT:

> Psalm 19:13. *Guilt and shame accompany sexual sin.*
> Proverbs 5:1-21. *Sexual sin causes scars and pain.*
> Romans 1:24-27. *Homosexuality and lesbianism are sins.*
> Romans 6:1-14. *Believers should not be involved in
>   sexual sin.*
> 1 Corinthians 3:19-20. *God doesn't care if "everybody's
>   doing it."*
> 1 Corinthians 6:13-20. *Run from sexual sin.*
> Ephesians 5:3-4. *Stay pure.*
> 1 Timothy 6:11-12. *Run from temptation.*
> 2 Peter 3:14. *Say no to premarital sex.*

S I N

No Little Sins

Bible Reading: Genesis 3:17-24; 4:8-12

Key Verse: *Now Cain talked with Abel his brother; and it came to
pass, when they were in the field, that Cain rose up against
Abel his brother and killed him.* Genesis 4:8, NKJV

Adam and Eve's disobedience brought sin into the
human race. They may have thought their sin—eating

a "harmless" piece of fruit—wasn't very bad, but notice how quickly their sinful nature developed in the lives of their children. Simple disobedience degenerated into outright murder. Adam and Eve acted only against God, but Cain acted against both God and man. A small sin has a way of growing out of control. Let God help you with your "little" sins, before they turn into tragedies.

Learn from Your Mistakes

Bible Reading: 1 Kings 15:25–16:7

Key Verse: *He did what was evil in the sight of the LORD, walking in the way of Jeroboam and in the sin that he caused Israel to commit.* 1 Kings 15:34, NRSV

God destroyed Jeroboam's descendants for their flagrant sins, and yet King Baasha repeated the same mistakes. He did not learn from the example of those who went before him. He did not stop to think that his sin would be punished. Make sure you learn the lessons from your own past, the lives of others, and the lives of those whose stories are told in the Bible. Don't repeat their mistakes.

Sin Is Serious

Bible Reading: Ezra 9:5-15

Key Verse: *But now, O our God, what can we say after this? For we have disregarded [your] commands.* Ezra 9:10, NIV

After learning about the sins of the people, Ezra fell to his knees in prayer. His heartfelt prayer provides a good perspective on sin. He recognized: (1) that sin is serious (9:6); (2) that no one sins without affecting others (9:7); (3) that he was not sinless, although he didn't have a heathen wife (9:10ff.); and (4) that God's love and mercy had spared the nation when they did nothing to deserve it (9:8-9, 15). It is easy to view sin lightly in a world that sees sin as inconsequential, but we should view sin as seriously as Ezra did.

On the Edge

Bible Reading: Psalm 38:1-22

Key Verse: *For I am ready to fall, and my sorrow is continually before me.* Psalm 38:17, NASB

In David's confession of sin, he acknowledged that he was "ready to fall." No matter how hard we try to follow God, we are sinners by nature and sin often. We stand on the verge of sin as if we were walking along the edge of a cliff and could fall at any moment. Those who think they are beyond sin are sure to fall. Therefore, the first step toward avoiding sin is to acknowledge our tendency to sin. Only then will we be ready to say no.

Friendly with Sin

Bible Reading: Proverbs 1:1-19

Key Verse: *My child, if sinners entice you, do not consent.* Proverbs 1:10, NRSV

Sin is attractive because it offers a quick route to prosperity and makes us feel like one of the crowd. When we go along with others and refuse to listen to the truth, our own appetites become our masters, and we'll do anything to satisfy them. There is something hypnotic and intoxicating about wickedness. One sin leads us to want to sin more. Sinful behavior seems more exciting than the "boring" Christian life. Don't be deceived—sin is dangerous and deadly. We must learn to make choices, not on the basis of flashy appeal or short-range pleasure, but in view of the long-range effects. Sometimes this means steering clear of people who want to draw us into activities that we know are wrong. We can't be friendly with sin and expect our lives to remain unaffected. Turn and run—this is not cowardly. Rather, it is extremely brave.

When You Want to Do Right

Bible Reading: Romans 7:15-25

Key Verse: *I do not understand my own actions. For I do not do what I want, but I do the very thing I hate.* Romans 7:15, NRSV

This is more than the cry of one desperate man—
it describes the experience of any Christian struggling against sin. We must never underestimate the
power of sin. Satan is a crafty tempter, and we have a
great ability to make excuses. Instead of trying to
overcome sin with human willpower, we must take
hold of the tremendous power of Christ that is available to us. This is God's provision for victory over sin.
He sends the Holy Spirit to live in us and give us
power. When we fall, he lovingly reaches out to us
and helps us up.

CHECK IT OUT:

> Psalm 119:25. *Let God's Word keep you from sin.*
> Isaiah 40:28-31. *Turn to Christ to avoid sin.*
> Matthew 23:23-24. *Don't seek to please people.*
> Matthew 25:45. *Refusing to help when you are able is sin.*
> John 4:10-14. *Read God's Word daily.*
> James 4:17. *It is sin to know what is right and not do it.*

SUCCESS

Doing It Your Way

Bible Reading: 2 Samuel 5:19-25

Key Verse: *And David did so, as the* LORD *commanded him; and he drove back the Philistines from Geba as far as Gezer.*
                                        2 Samuel 5:25, NKJV

David fought his battles the way God instructed him.
In each instance he (1) asked if he should fight or not;
(2) followed instructions carefully; and (3) gave God
the glory. We can err in our "battles" by ignoring these
steps and instead doing what we want without considering God's will, doing things our way and ignoring
advice in the Bible or from wise people, and taking the
glory ourselves or giving it to someone else without acknowledging the help we received from God. All of
these responses are sin, but doing it God's way brings
real success.

What Really Matters

Bible Reading: 1 Chronicles 5:24-25

Key Verse: *But they were unfaithful to the God of their fathers and prostituted themselves to the gods of the peoples of the land, whom God had destroyed before them.*

1 Chronicles 5:25, NIV

As warriors and leaders, these men had established excellent reputations for their great skill and leadership qualities. But in God's eyes they failed in the most important quality—putting God first in their lives. If you try to measure up to society's standards for fame and success, you will be in danger of neglecting true success—pleasing and obeying God. In the end, God alone examines our hearts and determines our success.

What's in Your Heart?

Bible Reading: Job 21:1-34

Key Verse: *How often is the lamp of the wicked put out? How often does calamity come upon them? How often does God distribute pains in his anger?* Job 21:17, NRSV

Job refuted Zophar's idea that evil people never experience wealth and happiness, pointing out that in the real world the wicked do indeed prosper. God does as he wills to individuals (21:22-25), and people cannot use their circumstances to measure their own goodness or God's—they are not necessarily related. Success, to Job's friends, was based on outward performance. Success to God, however, is in a person's heart.

The Measure of Success

Bible Reading: Jeremiah 18:1-18

Key Verse: *But they will say, "It's hopeless! For we are going to follow our own plans, and each of us will act according to the stubbornness of his evil heart."* Jeremiah 18:12, NASB

In the world's eyes, Jeremiah looked totally unsuccessful. He had no money, family, or friends. He prophesied the destruction of the nation, the capital city, and the temple, but the political and religious leaders would not accept or follow his advice. No group of people liked him or listened to him. Yet, as we look back, we see that he successfully completed the work God gave him to do. Success must never be measured by prosperity, fame, or fortune, because these are temporal. King Zedekiah, for example, lost everything. God measures our success with the yardsticks of obedience, faithfulness, and righteousness. If you are faithfully doing the work God gives you, you are successful in his eyes.

Trust in God

Bible Reading: Zechariah 4:6-10

Key Verse: *He said to me, "This is the word of the LORD to Zerubbabel: Not by might, nor by power, but by my spirit, says the LORD of hosts."* Zechariah 4:6, NRSV

Many people believe that to survive in this world a person must be tough, strong, unbending, and harsh. But God says that we will succeed because of his Spirit, even though we are weak. The key words are "by my Spirit." It is *only* through God's Spirit that anything of lasting value is accomplished. The returned exiles were indeed weak—harassed by their enemies, tired, discouraged, and poor. But they had God on their side! As you live for God, determine not to trust in your own strength or abilities. Instead, depend on God and work in the power of his Spirit!

What Are You Putting into Your Life?

Bible Reading: Acts 20:18-35

Key Verse: *However, I consider my life worth nothing to me, if only I may finish the race and complete the task the Lord Jesus has given me—the task of testifying to the gospel of God's grace.* Acts 20:24, NIV

We often feel that life is a failure unless we're getting a lot out of it, like glory, fun, money, and popularity. But Paul thought life was worth nothing unless he used it for God's work. What he put into life was far more important than what he got out. Which is more important to you—what you get out of life, or what you put into it?

CHECK IT OUT:

Proverbs 10:7. *Be full of goodness.*
Proverbs 13:5. *Always hate lies.*
Proverbs 16:3. *Commit all your work to the Lord.*
Proverbs 17:27-28. *Speak less and listen more.*
Proverbs 19:8. *Love wisdom.*
Proverbs 19:22. *Be kind.*
Proverbs 22:4. *Be humble and respect God.*
Proverbs 28:13. *Admit your mistakes.*
Mark 9:33-37. *Jesus' view of success was different from the world's.*

(see also Achievements)

SUFFERING

God's Purpose

Bible Reading: Job 23:1-17

Key Verse: *For he will complete what he appoints for me; and many such things are in his mind.* Job 23:14, NRSV

Job wavered back and forth, first proclaiming loyalty to God and then calling God his enemy. His friends' words and his own suspicions were undermining his confidence in God. When affliction comes, it is natural to blame God and to think that our suffering must be divine punishment. But we must not assume that God is being hostile towards us. His purposes go deeper than our ability to grasp all that is really happening. While this sounds like a pat answer, it is the same answer God gave Job in chapters 38–41. We shouldn't demand to know why certain calamities befall us. Often we cannot or are not meant to know until later.

Ask for God's Help

Bible Reading: John 9:1-9

Key Verse: *Jesus answered, "It was neither that this man sinned, nor his parents; but it was in order that the works of God might be displayed in him."*   John 9:3, NASB

A common belief in Jewish culture was that calamity or suffering was the result of some great sin. But Christ used this man's suffering to teach about faith and to glorify God. We live in a sinful world where good behavior is not always rewarded and bad behavior not always punished. Therefore, innocent people sometimes suffer. If God took suffering away whenever we asked, we would follow him for comfort and convenience, not out of love and devotion. Regardless of the reasons for our suffering, Jesus has the power to help us deal with it. When you suffer from a disease, tragedy, or handicap, try not to ask, "Why did this happen to me?" or "What did I do wrong?" Instead, ask God to give you strength through the trial and offer you a deeper perspective on what is happening.

Trials and Sorrows

Bible Reading: John 16:19-33

Key Verse: *In the world you face persecution. But take courage; I have conquered the world!*   John 16:33, NRSV

Suffering doesn't just happen to bad people. God says that the rain falls on the just and the unjust. In addition, Jesus guaranteed his followers that they wouldn't escape suffering. When evil happens, believers may wonder if God sees or cares. They may run to God and ask why. But while believers may want answers from God for the suffering they experience, they must first remember that while it is OK to ask, God is not obligated to answer. Like Job, we must be content that God is in charge.

Second, we must remember that we live in a broken world of sinful people. Our world is in rebellion against God. As a result, evil runs rampant, and Christians are not immune to its effects.

Third, remember that we can be comforted in the knowledge that while the battle rages, the war is already won. Jesus has overcome the world; only we won't experience it until he comes again.

Fourth, God is more concerned with our holiness than with our happiness. While the Christian life brings unspeakable joy, we will still face hardships and trials during which we must learn to imitate Jesus. Finally, we must remember that when we hurt, God hurts. He knows and understands our pain. He loves us so much that he suffered the ultimate pain in dying on a cross for us.

When you hurt, remember God's incredible love for you. He knows, he sees, and he cares.

Helping Others

Bible Reading: 2 Corinthians 1:3-7

Key Verses: *Blessed be the God and Father of our Lord Jesus Christ, the Father of mercies and God of all comfort, who comforts us in all our tribulation, that we may be able to comfort those who are in any trouble, with the comfort with which we ourselves are comforted by God.*

2 Corinthians 1:3-4, NKJV

Many think that when God comforts us, our hardships go away. But if that were always so, people would turn to God only to be relieved of their pain and not out of love for him. We must understand that *comfort* can also mean receiving strength, encouragement, and hope to deal with our hardships. The more we suffer, the more comfort God gives us (1:5). If you are feeling over-whelmed, allow God to comfort you. Remember that every trial you endure will later become an opportunity to minister to other people suffering similar hardships.

Suffering's Benefits

Bible Reading: 2 Corinthians 4:8-18

Key Verse: *So we fix our eyes not on what is seen, but on what is unseen. For what is seen is temporary, but what is unseen is eternal.* 2 Corinthians 4:18, NIV

Our troubles should not diminish our faith or disillusion us. Instead, we should realize that there is a purpose in our suffering. Suffering, in and of itself, is not a privilege. But when we suffer because we faithfully represent Christ, we know that our message and example are having an effect and that God considers us worthy to represent him (see Acts 5:41). Problems and human limitations have several benefits: (1) They help us remember Christ's suffering for us; (2) they help keep us from pride; (3) they help us look beyond this brief life and its earthly comforts; (4) they prove our faith to others and weed out superficial believers; (5) they give God the opportunity to demonstrate his great power; (6) they strengthen our faith; and (7) they serve as an example to others who may follow us. Don't resent your troubles—see them as opportunities!

CHECK IT OUT:

Genesis 4:6-7. *Sin causes inner suffering.*

Job 16:1-6. *Be an encouragement to those who are suffering.*

Habakkuk 3:17-19. *Trust God through suffering.*

Matthew 16:21-26. *Christ's followers will endure suffering.*

Acts 5:41. *Suffering can be an honor.*

Romans 8:18-21. *Sin can cause suffering.*

Philippians 1:29. *Suffering for Christ's sake is a privilege.*

Hebrews 2:11-18. *Jesus can help us through suffering.*

1 Peter 2:21-24. *Respond to suffering as Christ did.*

(see also Problems)

TEMPTATION

No Rationalizing

Bible Reading: Leviticus 11:1-12

Key Verse: *Their flesh you shall not eat, and their carcasses you shall not touch. They are unclean to you.*

Leviticus 11:8, NKJV

God had strictly forbidden eating the meat of certain animals. To help the Israelites obey him and avoid temptation, he forbade even touching these animals. He wanted the people to be totally separated from those things he had forbidden. So often we flirt with temptation, rationalizing that at least we are technically keeping the commandment not to commit the sin. But God wants us to separate ourselves completely from all sin and tempting situations.

Ways to Overcome

Bible Reading: 2 Samuel 11:1-27

Key Verses: *Now when evening came David arose from his bed and walked around on the roof of the king's house, and from the roof he saw a woman bathing; and the woman was very beautiful in appearance. So David sent and inquired about the woman.* 2 Samuel 11:2-3, NASB

As David gazed from his palace roof, he saw a beautiful woman taking a bath, and lust filled his heart. He should have left the roof and fled from the temptation. Instead, he went farther by asking about Bathsheba. The results of letting temptation stay in his heart were devastating.

To flee temptation: (1) Ask God in earnest prayer to help you stay away from people, places, and situations that offer temptation. (2) Memorize and meditate on portions of Scripture that combat your specific weaknesses. At the root of most temptation is a real need or desire that God can fill. (3) Find another believer with whom you can openly share your temptations, and call this person for help when temptation strikes.

Build Your Defenses

Bible Reading: 2 Chronicles 14:1-8

Key Verse: *He said to Judah, "Let us build these cities, and surround them with walls and towers, gates and bars; the land is still ours because we have sought the LORD our God; we have sought him, and he has given us peace on every side." So they built and prospered.* 2 Chronicles 14:7, NRSV

Times of peace are not just for resting. They allow us to prepare for times of trouble. King Asa recognized the period of peace as the right time to build his defenses. He knew that it was too late to prepare defenses at the moment of attack. It is also difficult to withstand spiritual attack unless defenses are prepared beforehand. Decisions about what to do when temptations arise must be made with a cool head in the peace of untroubled moments, long before the heat of temptation is upon us. Build your defenses now before temptation strikes.

Everyone Gets Hurt

Bible Reading: Psalm 51:1-19

Key Verse: *Against You, You only, have I sinned, and done this evil in Your sight—that You may be found just when You speak, and blameless when You judge.* Psalm 51:4, NKJV

Although David sinned with Bathsheba, he said he had sinned against God. When someone steals, murders, or slanders, it is against someone else—a victim. According to the world's standards, sex between two "consenting adults" is acceptable because nobody "gets hurt." But people *do* get hurt—in David's case, a baby died and a man was murdered. All sin hurts us and others, and ultimately it offends God, because sin in any form is a rebellion against God's way of living. When tempted to do wrong, remember that you will be sinning against God. That may help you stay on the right track.

Where to Draw the Line

Bible Reading: Daniel 1:1-16

Key Verse: *But Daniel resolved not to defile himself with the royal food and wine, and he asked the chief official for permission not to defile himself this way.* Daniel 1:8, NIV

It is easier to resist temptation if you have thought through your convictions well before the temptation arises. Daniel and his friends made their decision to be faithful to the laws of their God before they were faced with the king's delicacies, so they did not hesitate to stick with their convictions. Sometimes we get into trouble because we have not previously decided where to draw the line. Before such situations arise, decide to hold fast to your convictions. Then when temptation comes, you will be ready and able to resist it.

The Power of Prayer

Bible Reading: Matthew 26:36-46

Key Verse: *Then He came to the disciples and found them sleeping, and said to Peter, "What! Could you not watch with Me one hour?"* Matthew 26:40, NKJV

Jesus used Peter's drowsiness to warn him about the kinds of temptation he would soon face. The way to overcome temptation is to be alert to it and pray. Being alert involves being aware of the possibilities of temptation, sensitive to its subtleties, and spiritually equipped to fight it. Because temptation strikes where we are most vulnerable, we can't resist it alone. Prayer is essential because God's strength can shore up our defenses and defeat Satan's power.

You May Have to Run

Bible Reading: 1 Corinthians 10:1-14

Key Verse: *No temptation has seized you except what is common to man. And God is faithful; he will not let you be tempted beyond what you can bear. But when you are tempted, he will also provide a way out so that you can stand up under it.* 1 Corinthians 10:13, NIV

In a culture filled with moral depravity and pressures, Paul gave strong encouragement to the Corinthians about temptation. He said: (1) Wrong desires and temptations happen to everyone, so don't feel you've been singled out; (2) others have resisted temptation, and so can you; and (3) any temptation can be resisted because God will help you resist it. God can help you resist temptation in many ways, some of which are: (1) recognizing those people and situations that give you trouble, (2) running from anything you know is wrong, (3) choosing to do only what is right, (4) praying for God's help, and (5) seeking friends who love God and can offer help in times of temptation. But when the temptation seems overwhelming, running is the first step to victory (see 2 Timothy 2:22).

The Snowball Effect

Bible Reading: James 1:12-27

Key Verse: *But each one is tempted when he is drawn away by his own desires and enticed.* James 1:14, NKJV

Temptation itself is not a sin. Remember that Jesus was tempted, but he never sinned (Matthew 4:1-11). Our sinful natures are easy targets for temptation because it acts on our evil desires. Temptation brings to life an evil thought that becomes sin as we dwell on that thought and allow it to become an action. Like a snowball rolling downhill, sin's destruction grows the more we let sin have its way. The best time to stop a snowball is at the top of the hill, before it is too big or moving too fast to control.

CHECK IT OUT:

Proverbs 7:1-5. *Keeping God's commands will help you avoid temptation.*

Matthew 4:1-11. *Jesus demonstrated how we can combat temptation.*

1 Timothy 6:11-12. *Take steps to avoid temptation.*

2 Timothy 2:22. *Run from temptation.*

Hebrews 2:16-18. *Jesus Christ is our example.*

2 Peter 2:9. *God can rescue you from temptation.*

THANKFULNESS

Only You Can Do It

Bible Reading: Leviticus 7:28-38

Key Verse: Say to the Israelites: "Anyone who brings a fellowship offering to the LORD is to bring part of it as his sacrifice to the LORD."
Leviticus 7:29, NIV

God told the people of Israel to bring their sacrifices of well-being personally, with their own hands. They were to take time and effort to express thanks to God. You are the only person who can express your gratitude to God and to others. Take time to express thanks both to God and to others who have helped and blessed you.

God's Gracious Gifts

Bible Reading: Numbers 11:4-23

Key Verse: Moses heard the people of every family wailing, each at the entrance to his tent. The LORD became exceedingly angry, and Moses was troubled.
Numbers 11:10, NIV

Dissatisfaction comes when our attention shifts from what we have to what we don't have. The people of Israel didn't seem to notice what God was doing for them—setting them free, making them a nation, giving them a new land—because they were so wrapped up in what God wasn't doing for them. They could think of nothing but the delicious Egyptian food they had left behind. Somehow they forgot that the brutal whip of Egyptian slavery was the cost of eating that food. Before we judge the Israelites too harshly, it's helpful to think about what occupies our attention most of the time. Are we grateful for what God has given us, or are we always thinking about what we would like to have? We should not allow our unfulfilled desires to cause us to forget God's gifts of life, food, health, work, and friends.

More than Just Thanks

Bible Reading: 1 Chronicles 16:7-36

Key Verse: *Oh, give thanks to the LORD! Call upon His name; make known His deeds among the peoples!*

1 Chronicles 16:8, NKJV

Does it ever seem that a simple thank-you to God is not enough to express your appreciation? Four elements of true thanksgiving are found in this song: (1) *remembering* what God has done; (2) *telling* others about it; and (3) *offering* gifts of self, time, and resources. Get into the habit of fully expressing your thanks to God.

Plenty of Praise

Bible Reading: Psalm 103:1-22

Key Verse: *Bless the LORD, all you works of His, in all places of His dominion; bless the LORD, O my soul!*

Psalm 103:22, NASB

David's praise focused on God's glorious acts. It is easy to complain about life. But David's list gives us plenty for which to praise God—his love, forgiveness, salvation, kindness, mercy, justice, patience, tenderness— we receive all of these without deserving any of them. No matter how difficult your life's journey, you can always count your blessings—past, present, and future. When you feel like you have nothing for which to praise God, read David's list.

CHECK IT OUT:

Psalm 92:1-6. *Unthinking people never give thanks.*

Psalm 138:1-5. *God answers prayer, so be thankful.*

Luke 17:11-18. *Always thank God for his blessings.*

Acts 3:7-11. *Your thankfulness brings praise to God.*

Ephesians 2:4-10. *Be thankful for salvation and God's grace.*

Colossians 3:15-16; 1 Thessalonians 5:16-18. *Always be thankful.*

Colossians 4:2. *Thank God for his answers to your prayers.*

TRUST

Trusting While You Wait

Bible Reading: Genesis 30:1-24

Key Verse: *Then God remembered Rachel, and God listened to her and opened her womb.* Genesis 30:22, NKJV

Eventually God answered Rachel's prayers and gave her a child of her own. In the meantime, however, she had given her servant girl to Jacob. Trusting God when nothing seems to happen is difficult. But it is harder still to live with the consequences of taking matters into our own hands. Resist the temptation to think God has forgotten you. Have patience and courage to wait for God to act.

Building Trust

Bible Reading: Genesis 50:1-9, 22-26

Key Verse: *My father made me swear an oath and said, "I am about to die; bury me in the tomb I dug for myself in the land of Canaan." Now let me go up and bury my father; then I will return.* Genesis 50:5, NIV

Joseph had proven himself trustworthy as Pharaoh's adviser. Because of his good record, Pharaoh was sure that he would return to Egypt as promised after burying his father in Canaan. Privileges and freedom often result when we have demonstrated our trustworthiness. Because trust must be built gradually over time, take every opportunity to prove your reliability, even in minor matters.

Don't Break Your Promises

Bible Reading: Numbers 30:1-16

Key Verse: *When a man makes a vow to the LORD or takes an oath to obligate himself by a pledge, he must not break his word but must do everything he said.* Numbers 30:2, NIV

Moses reminded the people that their promises to God and others must be kept. In ancient times, people did not sign written contracts. A person's word was as binding as a signature. To make a vow even more binding, an offering was given along with it. No one was forced by law to make a vow, but once made, vows had to be fulfilled. Breaking a vow meant more than just a broken trust—it meant a broken relationship. Trust is still the basis of our relationships with God and others. Thus a broken promise today is just as harmful as it was in Moses' day.

Trust God No Matter What

Bible Reading: Job 1:6-22

Key Verse: *In all this Job did not sin nor charge God with wrong.*
Job 1:22, NKJV

When reading the book of Job, we are given information that the characters of the story didn't have. Job, the main character of the book, lost all he had through no fault of his own. As he struggled to understand why all this was happening to him, it became clear that he was not meant to know the reasons. He would have to face life with the answers and explanations held back. Only then would his faith fully develop.

We must experience life as Job did—one day at a time and without complete answers to all of life's questions. Will we, like Job, trust God no matter what? Or will we give in to the temptation to say that God doesn't really care? Rather than doing this, trust God with your unanswered questions. His will is perfect, and, in the end, you will not be disappointed with him.

Trust God to Change Your Life

Bible Reading: Jeremiah 32:6-25

Key Verse: *You showed signs and wonders in the land of Egypt, and to this day in Israel and among all humankind, and have made yourself a name that continues to this very day.*
Jeremiah 32:20, NRSV

Trust doesn't come easy. It wasn't easy for Jeremiah to publicly buy land already captured by the enemy. But he trusted God. It wasn't easy for David to think that he would become king, even after he was anointed. But he trusted God (1 Samuel 16–31). It wasn't easy for Moses to believe that he and his people would escape from Egypt, even after God spoke to him from a burning bush. But he trusted God (Exodus 3:1–4:20). It isn't easy for us to believe that God can transform our lives when we see the mess we've made. But we must trust God. He who worked in the lives of biblical heroes is the same God who offers to work in our lives, if we will let him do it.

Trust God with Your Future

Bible Reading: Acts 27:1–28:31

Key Verses: *He lived there two whole years at his own expense and welcomed all who came to him, proclaiming the kingdom of God and teaching about the Lord Jesus Christ with all boldness and without hindrance.*
Acts 28:30-31, NRSV

One of Paul's most important journeys was to Rome, but he didn't get there the way he had expected. It turned out to be more of a legal journey than a missionary journey, thanks to a series of legal trials and transactions. These events resulted in Paul being delivered to Rome, where he shared the gospel in the most amazing places, including the palace of the emperor! Sometimes we feel frustrated because our plans don't work out the way we wanted them to. But God is never out of control. He knows how to work things out so that the results are even better than we expected. Trusting God with your plans is a surefire plan for success!

God Works All Things Together for Good

Bible Reading: Romans 8:24-39

Key Verse: *We know that all things work together for good for those who love God, who are called according to his purpose.*
Romans 8:28, NRSV

God works out all things—not just isolated incidents—for our good. This does not mean that all that happens to us is good. Evil is prevalent in our fallen world, but God is able to turn it around for our long-range good. Note that God is not working to make us happy, but to fulfill his purpose. Note also that this promise is not for everybody. It can be claimed only by those who love God and are fitting into his plans. Such people have a new perspective, a new mind-set on life. They trust in God, not life's treasures. Their security is in heaven, not on earth. They learn to accept pain and persecution on earth—not resent it—because it brings them closer to God.

CHECK IT OUT:

1 Samuel 17:34-37. *David trusted God.*
Psalm 18:17. *Trust God to deliver you.*
Psalm 34:4. *Trust God to free you from fear and worry.*
Psalm 54:7. *Trust God to help you in your troubles.*
Psalm 57:1-11. *Have confidence in God.*
Isaiah 40:12-15, 25-31. *Trust God to control your life.*
Matthew 11:1-6. *Trust Christ without doubting.*
2 Timothy 1:12. *God is trustworthy.*

(see also Doubts and Faith)

USING ABILITIES

Ordinary Things

Bible Reading: Exodus 4:1-17

Key Verse: *The LORD said, "Throw it on the ground." Moses threw it on the ground and it became a snake, and he ran from it.*
Exodus 4:3, NIV

A shepherd's staff was a three- to six-foot wooden rod with a curved hook at the top. The shepherd used it for walking, guiding his sheep, killing snakes, and many other tasks. Still, it was just a stick. But God used the simple shepherd's rod to teach Moses an important lesson. God sometimes takes joy in using ordinary things for extraordinary purposes. What are the ordinary things in your life—your voice, a pen, a hammer, a broom, a musical instrument? It is easy to assume that God can use only special skills, but he can also use your everyday contributions. Little did Moses imagine the power his simple staff would wield when it became the rod of God.

Everyone Is Unique

Bible Reading: Deuteronomy 33:1-25

Key Verse: *Now this is the blessing with which Moses the man of God blessed the children of Israel before his death.*
Deuteronomy 33:1, NKJV

Note the difference in blessings God gave each tribe. To one he gave the best land, to another strength, to another safety. Too often we see someone with a particular blessing and think that God must love that person more than others. Instead, we should think that God draws out in all people their unique talents. All these gifts are needed to complete his plan. Don't be envious of the gifts others have. Instead, look for the gifts God

has given you, and do the tasks he has uniquely quali-
fied you to do.

God Is Preparing You

Bible Reading: Judges 13:1-25

Key Verse: *And the Spirit of the LORD began to stir him in Mahaneh-dan, between Zorah and Eshtaol.*

Judges 13:25, NASB

Samson's tribe, Dan, continued to wander in their
inherited land (18:1), which was yet unconquered
(Joshua 19:47-48). Samson must have grown up with
his warlike tribe's yearnings for a permanent and set-
tled territory. Thus his visits to the tribal army camp
stirred his heart, and God's Spirit began preparing
him for his role as judge and leader against the Philistines.

Perhaps there are things that excite you. These may
indicate areas where God wants to use you. God uses a
variety of means to develop and prepare us: hereditary
traits, environmental influences, and personal
experiences. As with Samson, this preparation often
begins long before adulthood. Be sensitive to the Holy
Spirit's leading and the tasks God has prepared for you.
Your past may be more useful to you than you imagine.

Live to Honor God

Bible Reading: Isaiah 47:1-15

Key Verse: *You felt secure in your wickedness; you said, "No one sees me." Your wisdom and your knowledge led you astray, and you said in your heart, "I am, and there is no one besides me."* Isaiah 47:10, NRSV

Caught up in the pursuit of power and pleasure, Babylon believed in its own greatness and claimed to be
the *only* power on earth. Babylon felt completely
secure. Nebuchadnezzar, its king, called himself
"god," but the true God taught him a powerful lesson
by taking everything away from him (Daniel 4:27-37).
Our society is addicted to pleasure and power, but

these can pass away quickly. Look at your own life, and ask yourself how you can be more responsible with the talents and possessions God has given you. How can you use your life for God's honor rather than for your own?

What Are You Doing with What You Have?

Bible Reading: Matthew 25:14-30

Key Verse: *To one he gave five talents of money, to another two talents, and to another one talent, each according to his ability.* Matthew 25:15, NIV

The master divided the money up among his servants according to their abilities—no one received more or less money than he could handle. If a servant failed in his master's assignment, his excuse could not be that he was overwhelmed. Failure could come only from laziness or hatred for the master. Money, as used here, represents any kind of resource we are given. God gives us time, abilities, talents, and other resources that he expects us to invest wisely until he returns. We are responsible to use well what God has given us. The issue is not how much we have, but what we do with what we have.

Effectively Using Gifts

Bible Reading: Romans 12:1-13

Key Verse: *We have many members in one body, but all the members do not have the same function.* Romans 12:4, NKJV

God gives us gifts so we can build up his church. To use them effectively, we must (1) realize that all gifts and abilities come from God; (2) understand that not everyone has the same gifts; (3) know who we are and what we do best; (4) dedicate our gifts to God's service and not to our personal success; and (5) be willing to spend our gifts generously, not holding back anything from God's service.

Body Life

Bible Reading: 1 Corinthians 12:1-31

Key Verse: *Now you are the body of Christ, and each one of you is a part of it.* 1 Corinthians 12:27, NIV

Using the analogy of the body, Paul emphasizes the importance of each church member. If a seemingly insignificant part is taken away, the whole body becomes less effective. Thinking that your gift is more important than someone else's is spiritual pride. We should not look down on those who seem unimportant, and we should not be jealous of others who have impressive gifts. Instead, we must use the gifts we have been given and encourage others to use theirs. If we don't, the body of believers will be less effective.

CHECK IT OUT:

Judges 15:3-8. *Don't use your gifts to do evil.*
Daniel 2:19-30. *Daniel gave God credit.*
Luke 12:48. *Gifted people have great responsibility.*
Romans 12:6-8. *Discover your abilities; then use them well.*
1 Corinthians 12:1-11. *Discover your spiritual gifts.*
2 Corinthians 1:21-22. *All believers have gifts.*
1 Timothy 4:14-16. *Use gifts and abilities for God.*

VALUES

Keeping God's Standards

Bible Reading: Genesis 19:1-26

Key Verse: *When he hesitated, the men grasped his hand and the hands of his wife and of his two daughters and led them safely out of the city, for the Lord was merciful to them.*

Genesis 19:16, NIV

Lot had lived so long—and was so content—among ungodly people that he was no longer a believable witness for God. He had allowed his environment to shape him, rather than he shaping his environment. Lot had compromised to the point that he was almost useless to God. When he finally made a stand, nobody listened. Have you also become useless to God because you are too much like your environment? To make a difference, you must first decide to be different in what you believe and how you act.

Where's Your Loyalty?

Bible Reading: Exodus 34:5-14

Key Verse: *For you shall worship no other god, for the LORD, whose name is Jealous, is a jealous God.*

Exodus 34:14, NKJV

God told the Israelites not to compromise with the sinful people around them, but to give their absolute loyalty and exclusive devotion to him. As we compromise, our sensitivity to sin becomes dulled. Are you beginning to accept lower standards regarding the things you do or think about? This could lead to a downhill slide you won't be able to stop. The way you act shows where your true allegiance is.

Stand for What's Right

Bible Reading: 2 Samuel 3:1-11

Key Verse: *Ish-Bosheth did not dare to say another word to Abner, because he was afraid of him.* 2 Samuel 3:11, NIV

Ish-bosheth was right to speak out against Abner's behavior, but he didn't have the moral strength to maintain his authority. Lack of moral backbone became the root of Israel's troubles over the next four centuries. Only four of the next forty kings of Israel were called "good." It takes courage and strength to stand firm in your convictions and confront wrongdoing in the face of opposition. When you believe something is wrong, do not let yourself be talked out of your position. Firmly attack the wrong, and uphold the right.

Stand Out for God

Bible Reading: Daniel 3:1-30

Key Verse: *There are certain Jews whom you have appointed over the administration of the province of Babylon, namely Shadrach, Meshach and Abed-nego. These men, O king, have disregarded you; they do not serve your gods or worship the golden image which you have set up.* Daniel 3:12, NASB

Why didn't the three men just bow to the image and tell God that they didn't mean it? They had determined never to worship another god, and they courageously took their stand. As a result, they were condemned and led away to be executed. They did not know whether they would be delivered from the fire. All they knew was that they would not bow to an idol. Are you ready to take a stand for God, no matter what? When you stand for God, you will stand out. It may be painful, and it may not always have a happy ending. Like Shadrach, Meshach, and Abed-nego, be prepared to say, "If he delivers me, or if he doesn't, I will serve only God."

CHECK IT OUT:

> 2 Chronicles 13:8. *Wrong values will defeat you.*
> Ezra 7:10. *Let God's Word shape your values.*
> Jeremiah 9:23-24. *Only one thing is of true value.*

Luke 9:26. *Jesus is ashamed of wrong values.*

John 16:20. *The world doesn't value Jesus Christ.*

1 Corinthians 6:18-20. *Strong values lead us away from sin.*

Philippians 1:9-11. *Learn right from wrong.*

Philippians 1:20-24. *Your values determine your life.*

WISDOM
Ask for Wisdom

Bible Reading: 1 Kings 3:3-10

Key Verse: *Give your servant therefore an understanding mind to govern your people, able to discern between good and evil; for who can govern this your great people?*

1 Kings 3:9, NRSV

When given a chance to have anything in the world, Solomon asked for wisdom, in order to lead well and to make right decisions. Notice that Solomon asked for wisdom to carry out his job. He did not ask God to do the job for him. We should not ask God to do *for* us what he wants to do *through* us. Instead we should ask God to give us the wisdom to know what to do and the courage to follow through on it (James 1:5).

You Don't Have to Be Old to Be Wise

Bible Reading: 2 Chronicles 34:1-11

Key Verse: *For in the eighth year of his reign, while he was still young, he began to seek the God of his father David; and in the twelfth year he began to purge Judah and Jerusalem of the high places, the wooden images, the carved images, and the molded images.*

2 Chronicles 34:3, NKJV

In Josiah's day, boys were considered men at age twelve. By sixteen, Josiah understood the responsibility of his office. Even at this young age he showed greater wisdom than many of the older kings who had come before him, because he decided to seek the Lord God and his wisdom. Clearly, wisdom from God is not the exclusive possession of the old. Young people may also be wise enough to fill spiritual leadership positions. Paul counseled Timothy to not let anyone think little of him because of his youth (1 Timothy 4:12). If God has given

you wisdom and spiritual insight, use it in his service
regardless of your age.

God Is the Source of Wisdom

Bible Reading: Job 28:1-28

Key Verse: *And he said to humankind, "Truly, the fear of the Lord,
that is wisdom; and to depart from evil is
understanding."*   Job 28:28, NRSV

People can perform all kinds of technological wonders.
They can find stars invisible to the eye, they can visit space,
they can store volumes of information on a microchip. But
even the greatest scientists, on their own, are at a loss to discover wisdom for their daily lives. Only God can show them
where to look to find wisdom because he is the source of
wisdom. True wisdom is having God's perspective on life. As
the Creator of life, only he knows what is best for his creation. It is fruitless for us to try to become wise merely
through our own observations and efforts, because God
alone sees the greater purpose for his world.

Applying What You Know

Bible Reading: Psalm 119:96-106

Key Verse: *Your word is a lamp to my feet and a light to my path.*
                    Psalm 119:105, NKJV

Intelligent or experienced people are not necessarily
wise. That's because true wisdom is not found in amass-
ing knowledge. Rather, it is *applying* knowledge in a life-
changing way. God's Word is full of life-changing
knowledge that can make us wise—wiser than our enemies, wiser than any teachers who ignore it. But this
knowledge only becomes wisdom when we allow what
God teaches us to make a difference in our lives.

The Process of Gaining Wisdom

Bible Reading: Proverbs 2:1-10; 3:1-26

Key Verse: *For the LORD gives wisdom; from His mouth come
knowledge and understanding.*   Proverbs 2:6, NASB

People don't develop all aspects of wisdom at once. For example, some people have more insight than discretion, while others have more knowledge than common sense. Rather, wisdom comes through a constant process of growth. First, we must trust and honor God. Second, we must realize that the Bible reveals God's wisdom to us. Third, we must make a lifelong series of right choices. Fourth, when we make sinful or mistaken choices, we must learn from our errors. Pray for all aspects of wisdom and seek to develop them in your life.

Respect the Wisdom of Older People

Bible Reading: Luke 2:24-38

Key Verse: *There was also a prophetess, Anna, the daughter of Phanuel, of the tribe of Asher. She was very old.*

Luke 2:36, NIV

Although Simeon and Anna were very old, they still hoped to see the Messiah. Led by the Holy Spirit, they were among the first to bear witness to Jesus. In the Jewish culture, elders were respected, so Simeon's and Anna's prophecies carried extra weight. Our society, however, values youthfulness over wisdom, and potential contributions by the elderly are often ignored. As Christians, we should reverse those values whenever we can. Encourage older people to share their wisdom and experience. Listen carefully when they speak. Offer them your friendship, and help them find ways to continue to serve God.

CHECK IT OUT:

Deuteronomy 34:9. *Joshua gained wisdom.*
Psalm 119:97-104. *Read your Bible and gain wisdom.*
Proverbs 1:7-9. *Fearing the Lord is the first step toward wisdom.*
Proverbs 8:1-36. *Wisdom gives life-sustaining advice.*
Proverbs 9:9-12. *Wisdom is its own reward.*
Acts 7:9-15. *Joseph was given great wisdom from God.*
Romans 11:33. *God's wisdom is beyond our comprehension.*

1 Corinthians 1:18-25; 3:19. *God's wisdom seems foolish to the world.*

James 1:5. *Ask God for wisdom.*

James 3:17-18. *Wisdom brings peace.*

WITNESSING

Recognize the Opportunities

Bible Reading: Genesis 40:1-8; 41:1-16

Key Verse: *Joseph answered Pharaoh, "It is not I; God will give Pharaoh a favorable answer."* Genesis 41:16, NRSV

When the subject of dreams came up, Joseph focused everyone's attention on God. Rather than using the situation to make himself look good, he turned it into a powerful witness for the Lord. One secret of effective witnessing is to recognize opportunities to relate God to the other person's experience. When the opportunity arises, we must have the courage to speak, as Joseph did.

Not Everyone Will Believe

Bible Reading: Exodus 9:13-35

Key Verse: *But when Pharaoh saw that the rain and the hail and the thunder had ceased, he sinned again and hardened his heart, he and his servants.* Exodus 9:34, NASB

At times you may get discouraged by those who consistently refuse to believe the truth of the gospel. When this happens, you must realize that not everyone is going to believe the message and that you are not responsible for their refusal. Like Pharaoh, who constantly and repeatedly hardened his heart against God's clear words and messages in the plagues, some people will remain unmoved by your witness. Your best tactic is to continue to show Christ's love and to pray for those people. Then leave the rest in God's hands.

Good News Won't Wait

Bible Reading: 2 Kings 7:1-20

Key Verse: *Then they said to one another, "What we are doing is wrong. This is a day of good news; if we are silent and wait until the morning light, we will be found guilty; therefore let us go and tell the king's household."*

2 Kings 7:9, NRSV

The lepers discovered the deserted camp and realized their lives had been spared. At first they kept the good news to themselves, forgetting their fellow citizens who were starving in the city. The Good News about Jesus Christ must be shared too, for no news is more important. We must not forget those who are dying without it. We must not become so preoccupied with our own faith that we neglect sharing it with those around us. Our wonderful news, like that of the lepers, will not "wait until morning."

What Do People Know about God from Watching You?

Bible Reading: Isaiah 43:10-13

Key Verse: *"You are My witnesses," says the LORD, "And My servant whom I have chosen, that you may know and believe Me, and understand that I am He. Before Me there was no God formed, nor shall there be after Me."*

Isaiah 43:10, NKJV

Israel's task was to be a witness, telling the world who God is and what he has done. Believers today share the responsibility of being God's witnesses. Do people know what God is like through your words and example? They cannot see God directly, but they can see him reflected in you.

Fulfill the Great Commission

Bible Reading: Matthew 28:16-20

Key Verses: *Go therefore and make disciples of all nations, baptizing them in the name of the Father and of the Son and of the Holy Spirit, and teaching them to obey everything that I*

*have commanded you. And remember, I am with you
always, to the end of the age.*   Matthew 28:19-20, NRSV

When someone is dying or leaving us, his last words are
very important. Jesus left the disciples with these last
words of instruction: They were under his authority;
they were to make more disciples; they were to baptize
and teach people to obey him; he would be with them
always. Whereas in previous missions Jesus had sent his
disciples only to the Jews (10:5-6), their mission from
now on would be worldwide.

Like the disciples, we are to go—whether it is next
door or to another country—and make disciples. It is
not an option but a command to all who call Jesus
Lord. All of us are not evangelists, but we have all
received gifts that we can use in helping to fulfill the
Great Commission. As we obey, we have comfort in the
knowledge that Jesus is always with us.

Pass Along Good News

Bible Reading: Mark 5:1-20
  Key Verse: *And he went away and began to proclaim in the
Decapolis how much Jesus had done for him; and
everyone was amazed.*   Mark 5:20, NRSV

This man had been demon possessed but became a living example of Jesus' power. He wanted to go with
Jesus, but Jesus told him to go home and share his story
there. If you have experienced Jesus' power, you, too,
are a living example. Are you, like this man, enthusiastic about sharing the Good News with those around
you? Just as we would recommend a good doctor who
cured a physical disease, we should tell others about
Christ, who saves us from our sin.

Who's Ready?

Bible Reading: John 4:27-38
  Key Verse: *Do you not say, "Four months more, then comes the
harvest"? But I tell you, look around you, and see how
the fields are ripe for harvesting.*   John 4:35, NRSV

Sometimes Christians excuse themselves from witnessing by saying their family or friends aren't ready to believe. Jesus, however, makes it clear that around us a continual harvest waits to be reaped. Don't let Jesus find you making excuses. Look around. You will find people ready to hear God's Word.

Reach Out

Bible Reading: John 12:37-50

Key Verse: *I have come as light into the world, that everyone who believes in Me may not remain in darkness.*

John 12:46, NASB

Jesus had performed many miracles, but most people still didn't believe in him. Likewise, many today won't believe despite all God does. Don't be discouraged if your witness for Christ doesn't turn as many to him as you'd like. Your job is to continue as a faithful witness. You are not responsible for the decisions of others, but simply to reach out to them. Don't hesitate to tell others about Christ because you fear that some will not believe you. At the same time, don't expect a unanimously positive response to your witnessing. Even if only a few believe, it's worth the effort.

What Do I Say?

Bible Reading: Acts 4:1-22

Key Verse: *We cannot stop speaking what we have seen and heard.*

Acts 4:20, NASB

It's true that witnessing can be difficult. You may wonder what to say or what to do if someone asks a question you can't answer. You may be really scared about witnessing, but think of it as learning any new skill—practice makes perfect. The point is, however, that you need to begin. The best beginning is to simply tell about what Jesus has done for you and what he means to you. You can't mess that up because it's your own personal story! You have a wonderful privilege to be able to share what you have learned and what God has done in your life. And if you're asked a difficult question, simply say, "That's a good question. Can I find out the answer and get back to you tomorrow?" Then be sure to follow up.

Identify with Your Listener

Bible Reading: Acts 22:1–23:1

Key Verse: *Since he wanted to find out what Paul was being accused of by the Jews, the next day he released him and ordered the chief priests and the entire council to meet. He brought Paul down and had him stand before them.*
Acts 22:30, NRSV

God used Paul's persecution as an opportunity for him to witness. Here even his enemies were creating a platform for him to address the entire Jewish Council. If we are sensitive to the Holy Spirit's leading, we will notice increased opportunities to share our faith, even in the heat of opposition.

CHECK IT OUT:

Jonah 3:1-10. *When God leads you to witness, do it.*
Matthew 5:14-16. *Light up your world by living for Christ.*
Matthew 9:9-13. *Share your faith with a lost world.*
John 15:27. *Tell your friends about Jesus.*
Acts 1:8. *The Holy Spirit gives strength for witnessing.*
1 Corinthians 9:22. *Win others for Christ.*
2 Corinthians 5:17-21. *You are Christ's ambassador.*
1 Peter 3:15. *Always be ready to tell people about your faith.*

WORRY

What Are You Worrying About?

Bible Reading: Genesis 7:1-16

Key Verse: *The animals going in were male and female of every living thing, as God had commanded Noah. Then the LORD shut him in.* Genesis 7:16, NIV

Many have wondered how this animal kingdom roundup happened. Did Noah and his sons spend years collecting them? In reality, the creation, along with Noah, was doing just as God had commanded. There seemed to be no problem gathering the animals—God took care of the details of that job while Noah was doing his part by building the ark. Often we do just the opposite of Noah. We worry about details in our lives over which we have no control while neglecting specific areas (such as attitudes, relationships, responsibilities) that *are* under our control. Like Noah, concentrate on what God has given you to do, and leave the rest to him.

How to Worry Less

Bible Reading: Philippians 4:4-19

Key Verse: *Do not be anxious about anything, but in everything, by prayer and petition, with thanksgiving, present your requests to God.* Philippians 4:6, NIV

Imagine never having to worry about anything! It seems like an impossibility—we all have worries on the job, in our homes, at school. But Paul's advice is to turn your worries into prayers. Do you want to worry less? Then pray more! Whenever you start to worry, stop and pray.

CHECK IT OUT:

Jeremiah 29:11. *Don't worry about the future.*
Matthew 8:23-27. *Let Christ calm the storms in your life.*
Matthew 10:19-20. *Turn to the Holy Spirit when you're worried.*
Matthew 10:29-31. *Don't worry—Jesus will take care of you.*
Matthew 14:25-33. *Don't look at troubles, look to God.*
Mark 4:35-41. *Place your confidence and trust in Christ.*
Luke 12:22-34. *Don't worry about clothing or food.*
1 Corinthians 10:13. *Don't worry about your problems.*

(see also Fear)

WORSHIP (SEE CHURCH)

YOUTH

Never Too Young to Obey

Bible Reading: 2 Kings 22:1-20

Key Verse: *And he did what was right in the sight of the LORD, and walked in all the ways of his father David; he did not turn aside to the right hand or to the left.* 2 Kings 22:2, NKJV

In reading the biblical lists of kings, it is rare to find one who obeyed God completely. Josiah was such a person, and he was only eight years old when he began to reign. For eighteen years he reigned obediently; then, when he was twenty-six, he began the reforms based on God's Law. Children are the future leaders of our churches and our world. A person's major work for God may have to wait until he is an adult, but no one is ever too young to take God seriously and obey him. Josiah's early years laid the base for his later task of reforming Judah.

Live Right

Bible Reading: Ecclesiastes 11:7-10

Key Verse: *Rejoice, young man, during your childhood, and let your heart be pleasant during the days of young manhood.* Ecclesiastes 11:9, NASB

We often hear people say, "It doesn't matter." But many of your choices will be irreversible—they will stay with you for a lifetime. What you do when you're young does matter. Enjoy life now, but don't do anything—physically, morally, or spiritually—that will prevent you from enjoying life when you are old.

Seek God When You're Young

Bible Reading: Ecclesiastes 12:1-8

Key Verse: *Remember now your Creator in the days of your youth,*

*before the difficult days come, and the years draw near
when you say, "I have no pleasure in them."*

Ecclesiastes 12:1, NKJV

Being young is exciting. But the excitement of youth
can become a barrier to walking closely with God if it
makes people focus on passing pleasures instead of
eternal values. Make your strength available to God
when it is still yours—during your youthful years. Don't
waste it on evil or meaningless activities that become
bad habits and make you callous. Seek God now.

Useful Youth

Bible Reading: John 6:1-15

Key Verse: *"Here is a boy with five small barley loaves and two
small fish, but how far will they go among so many?"*

John 6:9, NIV

In performing his miracles, Jesus usually preferred to
work through people. Here he took what a young child
offered and used it to accomplish one of the most spec-
tacular miracles recorded in the Gospels. Age is no barrier to Christ. Never think you are too young or too old
to be of service to him.

Set the Example

Bible Reading: 1 Timothy 4:11-16

Key Verse: *Let no one look down on your youthfulness, but rather in
speech, conduct, love, faith and purity, show yourself an
example of those who believe.* 1 Timothy 4:12, NASB

Timothy was a young pastor. In a culture that valued the
wisdom of the elderly over that of the youth, it was easy
for older Christians to look down on him. Paul knew this
and advised Timothy to earn the respect of his elders by
setting an example in his speech, life, love, faith, and
purity. Regardless of your age, God can use you. Whether
you are young or old, don't think of your age as a handicap. Instead, live so others can see Christ in you.

ZEAL

Famous Last Words

Bible Reading: John 13:31-38

Key Verse: *Peter asked, "Lord, why can't I follow you now? I will lay down my life for you."* John 13:37, NIV

Peter proudly told Jesus that he was ready to die for him. But Jesus corrected him. He knew Peter would protect himself by denying that he knew Jesus that very night (18:25-27). In our enthusiasm, it is easy to make promises, but God knows the extent of our commitment. Paul tells us not to think of ourselves more highly than we ought (Romans 12:3). Instead of bragging, demonstrate your zeal by persevering in your faith and growing in your knowledge of God's Word.

Off Target

Bible Reading: Philippians 3:1-11

Key Verse: *If anyone else thinks he has reasons to put confidence in the flesh, I have more: circumcised on the eighth day, of the people of Israel, of the tribe of Benjamin, a Hebrew of Hebrews; in regard to the law, a Pharisee; as for zeal, persecuting the church; as for legalistic righteousness, faultless.* Philippians 3:4-6, NIV

Our zeal can sometimes be misguided. Paul, for example, was a devout Jewish leader. Yet, in his religious zeal, he led the Jews in persecuting the church because he thought Christianity was heretical and blasphemous. But the Lord soon changed the direction of his zeal without reducing it.

Fading Light

Bible Reading: Revelation 2:1-7

Key Verse: *But I have this against you, that you have abandoned the love you had at first.* Revelation 2:4, NRSV

Just as when a man and woman fall in love, so also new believers rejoice at their newfound forgiveness. But when we lose sight of the seriousness of sin, we begin to lose the thrill of our forgiveness (see 2 Peter 1:9). In the first steps of your Christian life, you may have had enthusiasm without knowledge. Do you now have knowledge without enthusiasm? Both are necessary if we are to keep our love for God intense and untarnished (see Hebrews 10:32, 35). Do you love God with the same zeal you had when you were a new Christian?

CHECK IT OUT:

Numbers 25:1-13. *A priest demonstrates his zeal for the Lord's honor.*

2 Kings 10:1-27. *A future king shows his zeal for the Lord.*

Psalm 69:9. *A psalmist writes of his love for the house of the Lord.*

Proverbs 19:2. *Temper your zeal with knowledge.*

Isaiah 26:11. *The Lord has a great zeal for his people.*

John 2:17. *Jesus shows his zeal for his Father's house.*

Romans 10:2. *There is a zeal that isn't based on knowledge.*

Romans 12:11. *Never lack zeal for the Lord and his work.*

KEY VERSE INDEX

Old Testament

New Testament

STEPS TO PEACE WITH GOD

1. RECOGNIZE GOD'S PLAN—PEACE AND LIFE

The message you have read in this book stresses that God loves you and wants you to experience His peace and life.

The BIBLE says . . . *"For God loved the world so much that He gave His only Son, so that everyone who believes in Him may not die but have eternal life." John 3:16*

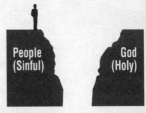

2. REALIZE OUR PROBLEM—SEPARATION

People choose to disobey God and go their own way. This results in separation from God.

The BIBLE says . . . *"Everyone has sinned and is far away from God's saving presence." Romans 3:23*

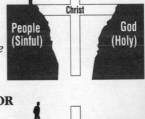

3. RESPOND TO GOD'S REMEDY—CROSS OF CHRIST

God sent His Son to bridge the gap. Christ did this by paying the penalty of our sins when He died on the cross and rose from the grave.

The BIBLE says . . . *"But God has shown us how much He loves us—it was while we were still sinners that Christ died for us!" Romans 5:8*

4. RECEIVE GOD'S SON—LORD AND SAVIOR

You cross the bridge into God's family when you ask Christ to come into your life.

The BIBLE says . . . *"Some, however, did receive Him and believed in Him; so He gave them the right to become God's children." John 1:12*

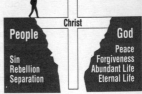

THE INVITATION IS TO:

REPENT (turn from your sins) and by faith RECEIVE Jesus Christ into your heart and life and follow Him in obedience as your Lord and Savior.

PRAYER OF COMMITMENT

"Lord Jesus, I know I am a sinner. I believe You died for my sins. Right now, I turn from my sins and open the door of my heart and life. I receive You as my personal Lord and Savior. Thank You for saving me now. Amen."

If you want further help in the decision you have made, write to:
Billy Graham Evangelistic Association, P.O. Box 779, Minneapolis, MN 55440-0779